and style

NTS

QUARRY

GLOUCESTER MASSACHUSETTS

mosaic art and style

DESIGNS FOR LIVING ENVIRONMENTS

JoAnn Locktov

QUARRY BOOKS

First published in the United States of America by:
Quarry Books, a member of
Quayside Publishing Group
33 Commercial Street
Gloucester, Massachusetts 01930-5089
Telephone: (978) 282-9590
Fax: (978) 283-2742
www.quarrybooks.com

Library of Congress Cataloging-in-Publication data available

ISBN-13: 978-1-59253-356-5
ISBN-10: 1-59253-356-6

10 9 8 7 6 5 4 3 2 1

Design: Peter King & Company
Cover image: Laurel True/David Bowman
Back cover images: Judi Brennan (right); Louis G. Weiner & Cindy D. Jones (left)

Additional Artists' Credits:
E.S. Baxter, 9
Linda Edeiken/Vincent Knakal, 8 (right); 10
Didier Guedj/Judy Guedj, 8 (middle)
Lucinda Johnson/Jeannie Schnakenberg, 94 (right)
Marcelo de Melo/Collection of Mrs. R. Braz, 94 (left)
Lucio Orsoni/Norbert Heyl, 8 (left); 144
Laurel Skye/Serge Hack, 5; 6 (bottom)
Laurel Skye/Mark Lufkin, 94 (middle)
Robyn Spencer-Crompton, 6 (top)
Karen Thompson/Rebecca Ford, 7 (top)
Karen Thompson/Russell MacMasters, 7 (bottom)

Printed in China

contents

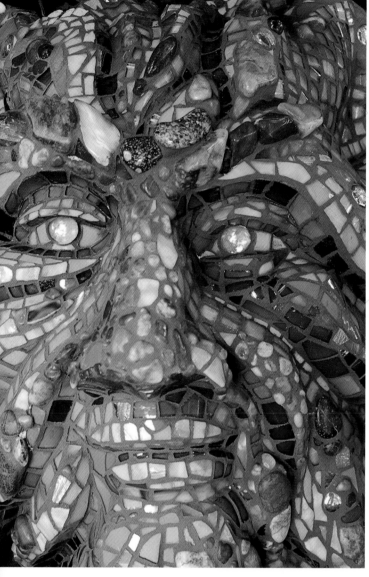

introduction

Mosaic Art and Style celebrates the integration of mosaics into the landscape of our daily lives. Not content to create fine art mosaics that hang on the wall in respectful silence, artists are creating architectural installations, sculpture, and furniture that enliven our living environments. The ancient Greek and Romans knew 3,000 years ago that mosaics were the perfect melding of functionality, durability, and beauty. Artists throughout the world are now redefining ancient traditions and transforming environments with individual fragments known as *tesserae*.

What does it mean to include mosaics in your living environment? Mosaic art can be applied to every surface imaginable, with imagination and a panoply of materials. The substances used in mosaics are as varied as the artists who create them. Color, texture, and personality will flourish where there was none before. Private living spaces will reflect identity, tradition, and even humor. A privy, dubbed *"See you there,"* is a site for both ecological composting and meditation. Using a mirror as the primary material, the mosaic outhouse reflects Vermont's seasonal dance of color. The flames of a fire glow inside a captivating marble surround, a noble family crest appears on a ceramic kitchen backsplash, a bathroom mirror radiates an obsession with shells, and a glass and cement howler monkey animates a garden.

Each project is a unique melding of personal taste. A formal parlor is transformed into a glamorous setting for a Victorian fantasy; a garden Buddha evokes serenity. Hotels and restaurants have also fallen under the spell of mosaics. From Venice, Italy, to Santa Fe, New Mexico, mosaics have been used to add opulence and historical perspective. As a guest, you can experience interiors that offer enclaves of mosaic art that capture a geographical spirit. In restaurants from Ravenna to San Francisco, diners feast amongst vibrant mosaic counters, walls, and tabletops.

Mosaics function as popular contenders for public art. Libraries, schools, and hospitals have been enhanced by mosaic projects that encourage solace, community spirit, and educational lessons. Refugee Safe Haven, a domestic-violence transition shelter, was the recipient of a mosaic mural. Originally meant to teach English to the women who stay there, it became apparent that there were words more important than "stop" and "go." The residents worked together to create a mosaic that defined seven words to live by. The *7 Wonders of Their World"* became Ambition, Dream, Peace, Courage, Power, Destiny, and Joy. The mural is a touchstone of hope rendered in mosaic. The desire for mosaic embellishment exists all over the world. Prior to the birth of the Internet, artists worked in relative isolation. Technology has provided the communication tools necessary for artists to share their work and techniques. Professional mosaic associations now exist in Italy, England, the United States, Brazil, Australia, France, and Japan. Hundreds of artists, all willing and anxious to explore methodologies, materials, and artistic endeavors, attend international conferences. This cross-fertilization of ideas makes for rigorous dialogue that inspires the rhythm of a vital artistic movement.

artist profiles

solomon bassoff and domenica mottarella

IN THE STUDIO OF FADUCCI, Solomon Bassoff and Domenica Mottarella sculpt the humble material of cement into a menagerie of fantastic animals. Cement, combined with an inlay of Italian glass or stone mosaic, creates a warm depth that invokes a striking visual and tactile experience. The materials come alive when the artists add natural mineral pigments and shape each sculpture into a captivating, naturalistic creation.

The inherent durability of the materials, coupled with additives, makes the mosaic art of Faducci resistant to frost and perfect for outdoor locations. The animals have also been known to pose for their owners in interior environments, often as sentries guarding a front door or peering out a window.

Sometimes it is the materials that inspire which animal will be created. With the discovery of pink iridescent glass, the flamingo series was born. Actual horns from animals that have died of natural causes find new life on a mosaic ram or impala. Menacing iguanas and crouching howler monkeys take their place alongside domestic dogs and cats.

The artists begin the basic structure by welding an armature and covering it in wire. Pigmented cement is then added and sculpted. Later, the mosaic elements are applied with thinset adhesive. The lifelike quality of the sculptures is enhanced by hand forming the cement until it is transformed into platelets on a turtle, feathers on a pelican, or fur on a ram. Solomon, who has been enamored with cement since his days as a general building contractor, developed and refined the cement-sculpting technique of Faducci.

‚ **SEA TURTLE**
Steel armature, pigmented cement, Italian glass tesserae, glass eyes
12" x 43" (30 x 109 cm)
Photo credit: Jim Beckett, Orin Bassoff

▲ **CORSICAN RAM**
Steel armature, pigmented cement, Italian glass tesserae, glass eyes, natural ram horns
42" x 34" (107 x 86 cm)
Photo credit: Solomon Bassoff, Orin Bassoff

‹ **FLAMINGOS**
Steel armature, pigmented cement, Italian glass tesserae, glass eyes.
58" x 38" (147 x 97 cm)
Photo credit: Solomon Bassoff, Orin Bassoff

‹‹ **CAT AND FROG**
Photo credit: Solomon Bassoff, Orin Bassoff

> **DOG WITH WINGS**
> Steel armature, pigmented cement, Italian glass
> tesserae, glass eyes
> 28" x 21" (71 x 53 cm)
> Photo credit: Solomon Bassoff, Orin Bassoff

With their extensive backgrounds in art, Bassoff and Mottarella wield a wide array of skills to form the particular expression unique to each creature. The choice of eyes can change the mood dramatically. In some cases, additional elements are necessary to complete the sculpture. A startled fawn requires a bee landing on his flank. A regal puppy is adorned with angel wings. It is with an intimate understanding and respect for wildlife that Bassoff and Mottarella create a covey of creatures both realistic and magical.

▲ **HOWLER MONKEY**
Steel armature, pigmented cement, gold leaf, Italian glass tesserae, glass eyes
32" x 26" (81 x 66 cm)
Photo credit: Jim Beckett, Orin Bassoff

▶ **FAWN WITH BEE**
Steel armature, pigmented cement, Italian glass tesserae, glass eyes
21" x 18" (53 x 46 cm)
Photo credit: Orin Bassoff, Solomon Bassoff

▶▶ **IGUANA**
Steel armature, pigmented cement, Italian glass tesserae, glass eyes
16" x 66" (41 x 168 cm)
Photo credit: Orin Bassoff, Jim Beckett

e. s. baxter

PHILADELPHIA-BORN E. S. BAXTER has merged his passions for architecture, painting, and mosaic in a culture without a word for *artist*. Living since 1990 in Tirta Gaugga, Bali, Baxter has integrated mosaics into his artistic palette, having been influenced by the mosaic edifices he found in Spain, Italy, and Turkey. However, it wasn't until he witnessed the mosaic sculptures of Niki de Saint Phalle that the inspiration took hold, and broken ceramic and glass took their place amongst brushes and canvas. In an extensive renovation of a rustic villa in eastern Bali, Baxter created a medley of historical elements in response to the client's request for an oriental theme. The arcade was built with Moorish brickwork and Mughal-style mirrored glass mosaic from Thailand via Belgium. The Thai temple-styled gazebo is topped with a Russian-inspired egg finial. Throughout the home, black and white is used as distinct accents, demonstrating a contemporary interpretation of *poleng*, the Balinese synthesis of opposites.

▲ PRIVATE VILLA: ROOFTOP GAZEBO, MOSAIC BALUSTRADE, AND ARCADE (DETAIL)

◂ PRIVATE VILLA: EGG FINIAL WITH A LIGHTNING ROD SPIRE
Ceramic tile mosaic applied over a cement shell with steel-framed hollow interior, green mirrored glass
8½' (2.6 m)

▸ PRIVATE VILLA: BALUSTRADE (DETAIL)
Iridescent ceramic tile over reinforced cast concrete
18' (5 m)

- ◄ PRIVATE VILLA: ARCADE (DETAIL)
  Brick over reinforced concrete core, mirror mosaic
  10' x 12' (3 x 3.6.m)

- ► PRIVATE VILLA: BATHROOM (DETAIL),
  MOSAIC SCULPTURE SHOWERHEAD,
  AND BILEVEL CEILING MOSAIC
  Ceramic, mirror
  32" (81 cm)

- ▼ PRIVATE VILLA: GAZEBO COLUMNS
  (DETAIL)
  Ceramic tile over reinforced concrete
  8½' x 5" (2.6 m x 13 cm) square

- ◄ PRIVATE VILLA: GARDEN BENCH
  Ceramic over plastered brick, bamboo
  40" x 80" x 24" (102 x 203 x 61 cm)

◂ FOR PAUL: MEMORIAL SCULPTURE WITH
ARMATURE AND FRAME SURROUNDING
SHATTERED GLASS
Reinforced cast concrete, ceramic mosaic
inscription and frame, glass.
Armature: 12½' x 51" x 55" (3.8 m x 130 cm x 140 cm)
Frame: 45" x 45" x 7" deep (114 x 114 x 18 cm)

▴ FOR PAUL (DETAIL)

At his own studio deep within the jungle, Baxter has created an extensive sculpture garden. Among the various works are thirteen mosaic pots of diverse pattern, shape, and color, balancing on brick pedestals situated along a mosaic path. The totemic *Pot Garden*, conceived with William Seeley, also pays homage to American composer and laser artist Paul Earls. A cast serpentine form embraces a mosaic frame containing glass shattered by Earls. The organic sculpture was created in Paul's memory and lends a sacred air to the lushly planted space.

Living in an isolated environment affords Baxter the solitude he craves to focus on his art. Materials are difficult to come by, and he often works within a limited color spectrum. Baxter sees this as a mixed blessing because he is forced to use texture to create interest rather than rely on the more conventional use of color. It is ironic that Baxter has chosen as his home a country that has no tradition of mosaic. It is, however, a culture that exalts artistic creation as a necessity of life.

◂ POT GARDEN: ONE OF THIRTEEN MOSAIC
POTS (DETAIL)
Ceramic over reinforced concrete
12" x 27" (30 x 69 cm)

◂◂ POT GARDEN AND MOSAIC PATH:
SEVERAL POTS AROUND NAME PLATE
(DETAIL)
Ceramic mosaic

▲ MOSAIC ROOM: OVERVIEW
Concrete block, cement, netting, ceramic tile
36' x 21' (11 m x 6 m)

▸ COUNTER (FLOWER DETAIL)
Ceramic tile, wood

judi brennan

IN TAUPO, NEW ZEALAND, there exists an enchanted mosaic living room, replete with an overstuffed sofa, floppy pillows, a spindly lamp, numerous windows, a comfy club chair, and a fireplace capable of generating smiles instead of heat. The room is Judi Brennan's homage to Antoni Gaudí, and like the Catalan artist, she has created this environment outside, among trees and foliage bathed in sunshine and able withstand winter's sub-zero temperatures.

▲ **LETTERBOX**
Ceramic tile, metal
3½' x 16" (1 m x 41 cm)

◄ **MOSAIC ROOM: FIREPLACE**
Concrete, netting, ceramic tiles
4' 7" x 5' 10" (1 x 2 m)

▼ **MOSAIC ROOM: LAMP**
Metal base, handmade mosaic tiles
6½' x 2½' (2 x 1 m)

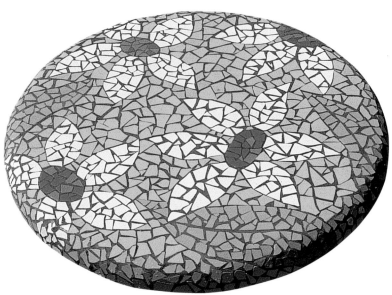

▲ MOSAIC ROOM: WALL (FLOWER DETAIL)

▶ MOSAIC ROOM: DAISY TABLE (DETAIL)
Metal, concrete, ceramic tiles
27" diameter (69 cm)

▼ MOSAIC ROOM: SOFA, WALL, AND LAMP
(DETAIL)

▲ MOSAIC ROOM: ARMCHAIR WITH VASE
Concrete block, netting, ceramic tiles

◄ MOSAIC ROOM: FLOOR MAT
Concrete, ceramic tiles
8' x 4½' (2 x 1 m)

In this garden living room, not a single right angle exists; the furnishings are formed with sensuous curves. Similar to the undulations found in Gaudi's *Parc Guell*, every piece in Brennan's capricious environment has a wavy contour. Cushions are fluffy, and the impregnable fireplace would be especially suitable in the Flintstones' Bedrock. An extravagance of primary color gives a cartoon quality to this delightful environment. The three-legged lamp could be a central character in a Dr. Seuss poem, and the sun never sets on the garden wall that frames the pin-striped sofa. A large mosaic carpet magically mirrors a section of the room, providing flooring that echoes the whimsical nature of the exterior room. A bright yellow armchair invites you to curl up with a good book. A table for two hosts oversize daisies that are charmingly defiant.

▸ MOSAIC ROOM: WINDOW VIEW
Concrete blocks, cement, netting, ceramic tiles

◂ MOSAIC ROOM: WALL WITH WINDOW
Concrete block, cement, netting, ceramic tiles

▾ MOSAIC FISH
Concrete, iron, terra-cotta tiles, wood
4' 4" x 8' (1 x 2 m)

◂ MOSAIC ROOM: VASE (DETAIL)

Brennan spent 30 years as a potter before discovering her passion for mosaics, possibly explaining her ability to finesse ceramics—a durable and hard material—into sculpture that appears cozy. Visitors to her 2½ acre Clay Art Studio and garden are amused and inspired with her creations, often returning to see what new adventure lies in store. Of her expressive under-taking, the self-proclaimed workaholic admits, "It's my never-ending project and a labor of love." Brennan's functional mosaic sculptures are the essence of extravagance and expression of an artist addicted to challenge.

marcelo de melo

IN THE IRREVERENT WORLD of Marcelo de Melo, mosaics are a launching point for his ideas and perceptions. Pushing the boundaries of traditional techniques, de Melo uses materials only as a means to an end, that end being the impassioned request to stimulate the viewer to the thoughts beyond the physical piece.

It is the idea behind the design that fascinates de Melo, as he claims, "It is what we do with mosaics that count." Studying and working in theater design in his native Brazil, de Melo moved to England, settling in Edinburgh, Scotland, in 1998, where he has achieved international recognition for his experimental mosaics. In his series of "structural mosaic works," the mosaic skins become much more than just surface embellishment; the shards define the structural integrity of the sculptures. In a rigid medium, de Melo has opted to create sensuous folds and curves, juxtaposing strength and fragility.

⌃ MIND YOUR OWN BUSINESS:
"STRUCTURAL MOSAIC WORK" SERIES
China, plaster, wire, grout
8½" x 13" x 10½" (22 x 33 x 27 cm)
Collection of Linda Allen

▲ MIND YOUR OWN BUSINESS:
"STRUCTURAL MOSAIC WORK" SERIES
(DETAIL)
Collection of Linda Allen

▸ PINK LEAF: "MOSAIC WORK" SERIES—
TOP VIEW
Vitreous glass, china, wire, plaster
14" x 12" x 8" (36 x 30 x 20 cm)
Collection of Mrs. R. Braz

◂ UNTITLED (69): "STRUCTURAL MOSAIC
WORK" SERIES
Souvenir mugs and plates, smalti, vitreous glass,
slate, plywood, wire, plaster
21" x 24" x 13" (53 x 61 x 33 cm)

◂ GROWTH (SIDE A): "STRUCTURAL MOSAIC
WORK" SERIES
Glazed ceramics, reclaimed crockery, smalti,
vitreous glass, slate, plywood, wire, plaster
23" x 15" x 17" (58 x 38 x 43 cm)
Collection of Mrs. Heath and Mr. Hargraves

▾ UNTITLED (69): "STRUCTURAL MOSAIC
WORK" SERIES (DETAIL)
Souvenir mugs and plates, smalti, vitreous glass,
slate, plywood, wire, plaster

▲ MODIFIED SEA CREATURES BATHROOM:
CEILING DETAIL
Glass tesserae, reclaimed crockery, glazed ceramics,
plywood, quarry tiles
Photo credit: Javi de Esteban

▶ MODIFIED SEA CREATURES BATHROOM
Glass tesserae, reclaimed crockery, glazed ceramics,
plywood, quarry tiles
Walls: 29' x 29' (9 x 9 m) Ceiling: 5' x 5' (2 x 2 m)
Floor: 5' x 5' (2 x 2 m).
Photo credit: Javi de Esteban

◄ **LOCH NESS BIKE (DETAIL)**
Glazed ceramics, reclaimed crockery, mirrors, bicycle
Photo credit: Javi de Esteban

▼ **LOCH NESS BIKE**
Glazed ceramics, reclaimed crockery, mirrors, bicycle
39" x 63" x 15" (99 x 160 x 38 cm)
Photo credit: Javi de Esteban

Questioning preconceptions is a recurrent them in de Melo's work. His *Modified Sea Creatures Bathroom* is at first glance an ocean-themed environment awash with waves of benign sea creatures. On closer inspection the creatures appear deformed—sea horses have two heads, and starfish have tails. The mosaic installation is a cryptic comment on genetic engineering, as well as on our ability to see what we want rather than what is. The bathroom has many admirers who have yet to discern the distorted creatures. Even the Loch Ness monster has provided a catalyst for de Melo's mosaic antics. Adding a third handle bar (representing the three humps) to a bicycle and using colors most often associated with Nessie, he has created a functional celebration of the poplar myth.

▶ **CLIMBING CROCKERY CUPBOARD**
Glazed tiles, reclaimed crockery, mirrors, MDF,
1950s plywood cupboard
70" x 34" x 15" (178 x 86 x 8 cm)
Photo credit: Javi de Esteban

Playfulness abounds in de Melo's work. He incorporates the elements of Pop Art by using souvenir mugs and the labels of ceramics manufacturers. His *Climbing Crockery Cupboard* places broken crockery on the outside of the furniture to contradict the purpose of the furniture, which is to display crockery on the inside of the cupboard. The broken crockery embedded in the mosaic surface creates a climbing wall with cups and plates providing the illusion of toeholds.

▲ NEOCLASSIC FIREPLACE
Glazed tiles, mortar, cardboard tubes, plywood
44" x 66" x 16" (112 x 168 x 41 cm)
Collection of Mr. G. Sugden, Edinburgh, Scotland
Photo credit: Javi de Esteban

◄ CLIMBING CROCKERY CUPBOARD
(DETAIL)
Photo credit: Javi de Esteban

The columns on an elegant neoclassical fireplace are made
with cardboard tubes, relinquishing the sophistication the style
demands for materials that substitute economy for purity.
De Melo creates mosaic art that perpetuates the need to
look beyond the obvious.

linda edeiken

IT WAS ONLY NATURAL that bead artist Linda Edeiken would find a unique way to incorporate her pointillistic materials into her mosaic art. While working with fine antique porcelains such as Spode, Limoges, and Imari, Edeiken was looking for a way to frame her damaged, yet delicate, "fragments of beauty" with a more elegant substance than traditional grout. Her innovative use of glass seed beads to fill the interstices between the china shards creates a dazzling effect, expanding the texture of her work. The mounds of reflective beads resemble a sumptuous feast of caviar, a sensuous replacement for the more humble, commonly used cement. She considers this seed-bead grout a hallmark and signature design element of her decorative pieces. However, she often uses colored cement grout for her functional pieces, in which the beaded grout would be too fragile.

◄ **YELLOW DOG BOX (DETAIL)**
Antique china, glass jewels, seashells, china figurine, seed bead grout
Photo credit: Vincent Knakal

▲ **GLASS BLOCK WINDOW WITH WATERMELON ROSE PLATE (ON WALL) AND COWRIE GARDEN PLATTER (ON TABLE)**
Photo credit: Vincent Knakal

◄◄ **ORIENTAL OVAL BOWL (DETAIL)**
Antique china, glass, seed bead grout
Photo credit: Vincent Knakal

▼ **COWRIE GARDEN PLATE (DETAIL)**
Antique china, glass, cowrie seashells, porcelain flowers, seed bead grout
Photo credit: Vincent Knakal

▸ HUMMINGBIRD VASE: "FROM MY GARDEN"
SERIES
Antique china, porcelain figures, tiles, glass
8" x 15" x 4" (20 x 38 x 10 cm)
Photo credit: Vincent Knakal

▾ BLUEBIRD VASE (DETAIL): "FROM MY
GARDEN" SERIES
Antique china, porcelain figures, tiles, glass jewels
Photo credit: Vincent Knakal

Influenced by her extensive travels abroad, and inspired by
Raymond Isadore and his eccentric home in Chartres, France,
Edeiken's contemporary expression of pique assiette (broken
plate) mosaics takes the tradition a step further. By treating
the space between the fragments as seriously as the shards
themselves, Edeiken has created a dual focus without hierarchy.
Broken and chipped antique dishes are transformed and emerge
from her Mad Platter Beaded Mosaics studio as joyous, decorative, and functional sculpture for the home.

▲ **BASKET OF SHELLS MIRROR (DETAIL)**
Seashells, china shards, glass, tile, beaded flowers
Collection of Carol Martin
Photo credit: Vincent Knakal

◀ **SCORPION SHELLS PLATTER (DETAIL)**
Antique china, glass, scorpion seashells, seed
bead grout
Photo credit: Vincent Knakal

Seashells are another motif found in her work. "I love shells and have been collecting them since I was five years old, when I spent summers in Atlantic City, New Jersey, with my family; they are some of the most beautiful forms in nature." Indeed, shells often act as exclamation points among the china shards. Ceramic "baskets" overflow with shells in aquatic cornucopias, with shell fans, shell bouquets, and shell centerpieces.

Edeiken's mosaics embody the festive use of saturated color that also characterizes her home and gardens in La Jolla, California. "I find the interplay of pattern and color exciting, and I choose my palette for a piece in much the same way that a quilter chooses fabric." Edeiken frequently adds sculptural embellishments of animals and petals, which create a lively menagerie of three-dimensional surfaces. Although her work is collected throughout the United States, it is, perhaps, in her own home that one can appreciate the ornate and radiant effect of living with her designs. The mosaics invite touch and celebrate a delightful array of resplendent hues and surfaces.

▲ DINING ROOM
   Photo credit: Vincent Knakal

▸ SPRING IN PURPLE MIRROR
   Antique china, porcelain pieces, seashells.
   26" x 24" x 6" (66 x 61 x 15 cm).
   Collection of Barbara Sivan.
   Photo credit: Vincent Knakal

▾ MASTER BATH WITH SPRING IN PURPLE
   MIRROR AND CHELSEA DAYDREAM PLATTER
   Photo credit: Vincent Knakal

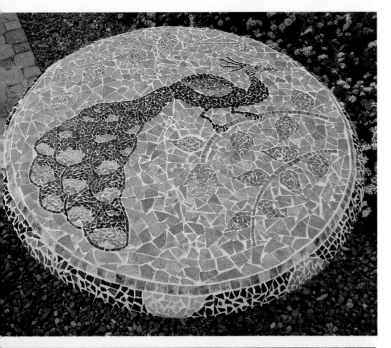

michelle enus

AFTER A SUCCESSFUL CAREER in the fashion industry, Michelle Enus followed her true passion: creating mosaics. Since 1989, she has enriched the lives of her clients with functional mosaic art. Enus integrates her training from the fashion world, explaining, "I am all about color. If it is up to me, there is lots of color and pattern." This is evident from her *Old Meets New* garden bench, in which she has created instant harmony by weaving antique tiles with contemporary ceramic, vitreous glass tesserae, and glass beads into intricate patterns of sun-bleached color. The bench is an amalgamation of vintage and modern and would satisfy any fashionista's craving for an imaginative silhouette. The same client requested an outdoor table, on which the exotic peacock with its vivid blues and greens melding with a terra-cotta background became the focus, and a mosaic base of dense foliage that emulates the stone path on which it is situated.

⬆ PEACOCK TABLE (DETAIL)
Photo credit: Andy Comins

▲ PEACOCK TABLE
Beach glass, ceramic tile
30" high x 42" diameter (76 x 107 cm)
Photo credit: Andy Comins

▸ OLD MEETS NEW GARDEN BENCH
Antique tiles, vitreous glass tesserae, glass beads
34" x 51" (86 x 130 cm)
Photo credit: Andy Comins

▸ OLD MEETS NEW GARDEN BENCH (BACK)
Antique tiles, vitreous glass tesserae, glass beads
34" x 51" (86 x 130 cm)
Photo credit: Andy Comins

The owners of Casa Bella asked Enus to help them re-create the atmosphere of their favorite island paradise of St. Bart's in their southern California home. Lending a tropical air to the hilltop location, palm trees and ocean and mountain views provide the stunning backdrop for the wave-inspired glass mosaic that borders the stairs and two planting areas.

▶ **CASA BELLA: CAESAR TABLE AND VASE**
  Beach glass, ceramic tile, glass shells, sea shells
  10' diameter x 30" high (3 m x 76 cm)
  Photo credit: Scott Fuller

▼ **CASA BELLA: CAESAR TABLETOP AND VASE (DETAIL)**
  Photo credit: Scott Fuller

The 10' (3 m) diameter Caesar table not only can seat fourteen diners comfortably, but it also becomes a dance platform at parties when the owners honor the St. Bart's tradition of dancing on top of the table. Enus created the large-scale vase centerpiece to complement the table's pattern and positioned it as a deterrent when dancing is not an option.

In the bronze kitchen backsplash, Enus worked in a more subtle, traditional vein. She recycled her client's existing tiles and added bronze tile to add continuity and meld the new mosaic insert with existing appliances and cabinet hardware. Enus works closely with interior designers, builders, and realtors throughout the United States to fashion mosaic creations that complement the taste and style of every client.

Enus's *Bouquet de Colores* embraces her visual sense of saturated color, enlivening a bathroom sink and backsplash with festive flowers. She applied a thin layer of cement to the counter, which is built of wood, and then painted it as the perfect neutral canvas to induce the stylized ceramic blooms to burst with pigment.

▲ **TRADITIONAL BRONZE KITCHEN BACKSPLASH**
Metallic bronze tile, ceramic tile
18" x 5' 6" (46 cm x 2 m)
Photo credit: Scott Fuller

▼ **BOUQUET DE COLORES SINK AND BACKSPLASH**
Stained glass, glass beads
20" x 17" (51 x 43 cm)
Photo credit: Lance Reynolds

▲ **LOUNGING LIZARD (DETAIL)**
Glass beads, cement, chicken wire, Styrofoam
17' (5 m)
Photo credit: Judy Guedj

▸ **GARDEN STEPS (DETAIL)**
Ceramic tile, glass beads, china
Photo credit: Judy Guedj

didier guedj

THERE IS AN EARTHINESS to the work of French-born artist Didier Guedj. His mosaics radiate a naïve pleasure with the world, often creating bucolic farm scenes at the request of his clients. Castaway items frequently become the pivotal inspiration for mosaic wonders. His *Lounging Lizard* was rescued from the side of the road and rebuilt with chicken wire, cement, and liquid foam. The sculpture was then encrusted in thousands of glass beads to replicate a lizard's scales. Guedj has contributed multiple projects to the Solano County Community Garden and Urban Farm Orchard. The community spirit found in public gardens propels Guedj into action.

▲ PASTORAL KITCHEN BACKSPLASH FEATURING A ROOSTER — BRAVO RESIDENCE
Ceramic tile. 3' x 1½' (1 x .5 m).
Photo credit: Judy Guedj

▼ PASTORAL KITCHEN BACKSPLASH (DETAIL)
Photo credit: Judy Guedj

The fascination for Guedj, a professional tile setter turned self-taught mosaic artist, is a spiritual awareness that guides his motives through daily meditation and prayer. Guedj is an Aquarius, and the ruler of this sun sign is the planet Uranus. According to Guedj, Uranus is a planet of awakening and rules not only in astrology but also for mosaics. Uranus is the planet responsible for allowing us to transition from an unconscious to a conscious state of mind. The analogy in mosaic art is the process of breaking and arranging inanimate materials to create involvement and expressive concern.

▲ BARNYARD KITCHEN MOSAIC (DETAIL)
Photo credit: Judy Guedj

◄ BARNYARD KITCHEN MOSAIC –
GRAGEDA RESIDENCE
Ceramic tile
8' x 1½' (2 m x 43 cm)
Photo credit: Judy Guedj

▼ KITCHEN ASTROLOGY TABLE
Ceramic tile
41" diameter (104 cm)
Photo credit: Pilar Reynaldo

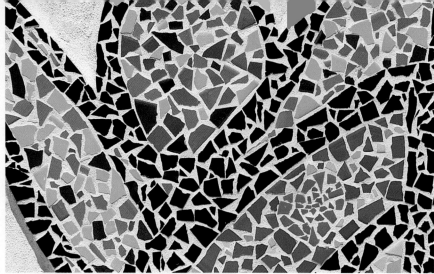

▸ **A HIGHER GOAL**
Ceramic tile
7' (2 m)
Photo credit: Judy Guedj

▲ **A HIGHER GOAL (DETAIL)**
Photo credit: Judy Guedj

▾ **SAILBOAT WITH FAMILY CREST (DETAIL)**
HUGH McCULLUM RESIDENCE
Ceramic tile
Photo credit: Judy Guedj

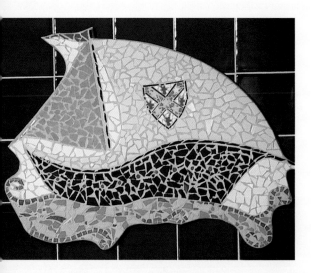

A spontaneous sketch on a coffee shop napkin resulted in the 7' (2.1 m) mural *A Higher Goal*. The ceramic figure adorns a cinder-block wall, a testament to the ability of humankind to aspire to its greatest potential despite the severity of life. Guedj's work often speaks to the human condition as he strives to "break away from traditional thought to effect change via the heart."

Sometimes it is Guedj's responsibility to discover exactly what his clients want in a mosaic. His process is simple: By asking what makes them most happy, he can determine the essence of a mosaic's content. A mosaic sailboat hoisting a family crest allowed a custom commission to reflect not only a favorite pastime but a traditional family icon as well.

◄ RAINBOW MURAL, SOLANO CANYON
COMMUNITY GARDEN AND URBAN FARM
AND ORCHARD (DETAIL OF KATIE FROM
IN KATIE'S WORLD)
Photo credit: Judy Guedj

▼ RAINBOW MURAL, SOLANO COUNTY
COMMUNITY GARDEN AND URBAN
ORCHARD AND FARM (DETAIL OF ZARK
FROM *IN KATIE'S WORLD*)
Photo credit: Judy Guedj

⩔ RAINBOW MURAL, SOLANO CANYON
COMMUNITY GARDEN AND URBAN FARM
AND ORCHARD (DETAIL OF LYNDY FROM
IN KATIE'S WORLD)
Ceramic tile
1½' x 2' (43 x 61 cm)

In Katie's World is populated by a joyous community of children designed by Judy, Guedj's wife and business partner. The entire *Rainbow Mural* reflects the diverse ethnicity of the neighborhood, as the life-size children cavort and play in their unique garden setting.

Guedj begins each project by remembering the words of the Indian holy man, Sri Sathya Sai Baba, "Heart is inside and art is outside." Guedj's aspiration is to reflect the most vital center of his being in the art that he is compelled to create.

lucinda johnson

AS AN ART STUDENT at the University of California in Davis, Lucinda Johnson received both her bachelor's and master's of fine art degrees studying under the tutelage of three of California's most significant modern masters. Wayne Theibaud trained Johnson in classical painting technique; his emphasis on basic mastery and art history gave Johnson her foundation. Her mentor, ceramist Bob Arneson, encouraged the mixing of different media. The irreverent Roy de Forest inspired Johnson's discovery of mixed-media constructions. Mosaic became the natural synthesis of the skills Johnson acquired in painting and ceramics. After a chance meeting with the widow of Millard Sheets (who produced extensive mosaics throughout the world in the 1940s, '50s, and '60s) provided Johnson with a treasure trove of smalti, she was on her way. In 2000, she moved to San Miguel Allende, Mexico, from Gualala, California. This change of scenery has inspired the exuberant burst of color apparent in her current work and enabled her to create larger commissions due to her ability to hire her neighboring campesinos from Ejido Los Lopez to assist in her studio.

Marine life is a significant theme in Johnson's work. Growing up with an oceanographer father, she spent most of her childhood near oceans and rivers, often collecting sea creatures in tidal pools. One of Anima Ceramic Design's most popular mosaic inserts, a combination of shells with a central crab motif, is sold internationally through Ann Sacks Tile & Stone. The mosaic is customized with different colors of smalti and ceramic glaze and has been used in more than 100 different sites in the United States, Europe, and Mexico.

The fanciful fish in her son's bathroom is a different interpretation of the mosaic insert. The colors were chosen to brighten a small space, and a bass replaces the crab. The Gualala River is immortalized in Johnson's own *River Bathroom*. Steelhead trout, frogs, salamanders, and crawdads are created in stoneware, swimming along a tide of Italian smalti.

⬆ **CRAB AND SHELL MOSAIC INSERT**
Stoneware, Italian smalti
18" x 19" (46 x 48 cm)
Photo credit: Jeannie Schnakenberg

▲ **CARIBBEAN SCENE (DETAIL)**
PRIVATE RESIDENCE IN NASSAU, BAHAMAS
Stoneware, tumbled smalti, Bizassa Opus Romano
Photo credit: Jeannie Schnakenberg

▸ **FISH AND SHELL BATHROOM**
Stoneware, Italian smalti, copper smalti
23" x 25" (58 x 64 cm)
Photo credit: Jeannie Schnakenberg

▸▸ **RIVER BATHROOM**
Stoneware, Italian smalti
14" x 80" (36 x 203 cm)
Photo credit: Jeannie Schnakenberg

▲ GUANAJUATO SUN (DETAIL)
Photo credit: Jeannie Schnakenberg

Johnson created the *Guanajuato Sun* mural for an indoor patio of a home in Mexico. The prevalent pre-Columbian Sun motif is a dazzling combination of ceramic and glass. The winsome features of the moons and suns add a naïve charm to the exultant palette of color.

In a Mexican colonial home, Johnson conceived and produced an elegant formal mosaic, which mirrors the original seventeenth-century carved mantle, adding flowers and gold smalti to heighten the reverence to the original inspiration over the kitchen stove.

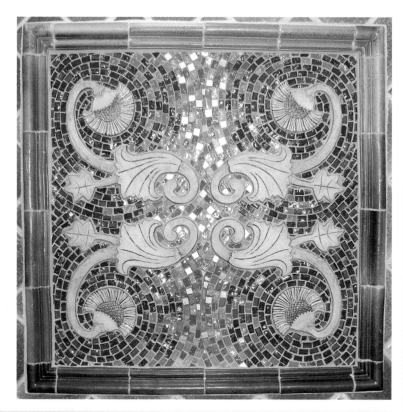

- ▾ MEXICO KITCHEN MOSAIC
  JAMES AND KAREN WITTLIFF RESIDENCE
  Stoneware, Italian smalti, gold smalti
  28" x 28" (71 x 71 cm)
  Photo credit: Jeannie Schnakenberg

- ◂ MEXICO KITCHEN MOSAIC (DETAIL)
  JAMES AND KAREN WITTLIFF RESIDENCE
  Photo credit: Jeannie Schnakenberg

- ◂ GUANAJUATO SUN
  Stoneware, Italian smalti, beach glass
  5' x 8' (1.5 x 2.4 m)
  Photo credit: Jeannie Schnakenberg

▲ OSTIAN SEA (DETAIL)
Semiprecious stone, marble, granite,
ebonized cherry wood
34" diameter (86 cm)
Photo credit: John Polak Photography

richard moss

WHEN RICHARD MOSS was a child, *National Geographic* magazine was printed in black and white. Surreptitiously, he tore out a coin-size photo of an Ostian mosaic. More than 20 years later, he found the photo in a box of childhood treasures. The torn and faded photograph motivated him to create the *Ostian Sea* table as testament to an art form that not only fascinated him as a child but became his life's work. In this table, he used stone from every continent, with the exception of Antarctica. The original monochromatic sea urchin became jasper and amethyst. It is fitting that an artist who speaks several languages and is continually inspired by his respect and study of global art history should make use of materials from around the world.

▾ OSTIAN SEA
Semiprecious stones, marble, granite, ebonized cherry wood
34" diameter (86 cm)
Photo credit: John Polak Photography

▲ BAROQUE HORSE SERIES
PRIVATE COLLECTION
Ceramic pique assiette, handmade tiles
28" x 22" each (71 x 56 cm)
Photo credit: John Polak Photography

▸ AMERICAN CROW
Marble, granite, formed copper support
16" diameter (41 cm)
Photo credit: John Polak Photography

▲ AMERICAN CROW (DETAIL)
Marble, granite, formed copper support
16" diameter (41 cm)
Photo credit: John Polak Photography

Moss works figuratively and naturalistically. His mosaic art displays an elegance and verisimilitude that is consistent with his notion that "the dignity that mosaic lends to its subject allows me to create a viewing lens through which one can see the familiar anew."

◂ CITYSCAPE, NEW YORK CITY
PRIVATE COLLECTION
Marble, granite, smalti, ceramic
34" x 22" (86 x 56 cm)
Photo credit: John Polak Photography

▾ GRAPE VINE MOSAIC (DETAIL)
LA CUCINA DE PINOCCHIO, AMHERST, MA
Ceramic pique assiette and handmade tile mosaic
28' x 1' (8.5 x .3 m)
Photo credit: John Polak Photography

In his homage to Florida's Panhandle in the National Endowment for the Arts public art mosaic *A Pure Land*, Moss treats the indigenous animals and foliage with the same reverence many would reserve for religious icons. His choice of black-and-white marble and granite belie the complicated issues that prevail in this Florida region. By bursting out of the geometric constraints, he both achieves movement and evokes a timelessness with this fragment of Florida that Disney has not yet paved.

Nasrid Faith was inspired by a time when science, math, and religion were seamlessly intertwined. It focused on a central image and grew organically, one piece at a time. Although Moss could have used a water saw for precision and time savings, he chose to work by hand, letting the design develop into a hypnotic whole. It is clear the process of creation—sketching, drawing, designing a cartoon, and fabricating the mosaic—are intrinsic elements, equally as important as the finished work.

The name of his firm, Equipment of Culture, came from reading the dictionary and discovering this second definition of *furniture*. It is impossible to imagine the word *culture* not embodying Moss's work because erudition and discernment govern all his mosaic art.

▸ A PURE LAND: DEER (DETAIL)
NEAL CIVIC CENTER, TALLAHASSEE,
FLORIDA
Marble, granite
Photo credit: Lori Hamilton

▸ A PURE LAND
NEAL CIVIC CENTER, TALLAHASSEE,
FLORIDA
Marble, granite
17' x 24' (5 x 7 m)
Photo credit: Lori Hamilton

◄ NASRID FAITH (DETAIL)
Marble, granite, ebonized cherry wood
34" diameter (86 cm)
Photo credit: John Polak Photography

▾ NASRID FAITH
Marble, granite, ebonized cherry wood
34" diameter (86 cm)
Photo credit: John Polak Photography

lucio orsoni

IF YOU LIGHT A MATCH and hold it up to a mosaic created with Orsoni smalti, the flame becomes smaller. Unlike other glass, which reflects the light that shines upon it, the material produced since 1888 by the Orsoni factory captures the light and swallows it whole.

This unique property has made Orsoni smalti the most revered in the world. The rich opacity of color wrought by traditional techniques distinguishes this material.

Lucio Orsoni, the great-grandson of founder Angelo Orsoni, has achieved international recognition for his sublime mosaics, executed in monochromatic designs, featuring shades of gold. Manufacturer and artist, Orsoni is now a maestro, completing his lifelong desire to teach the art of mosaic and house students under the same roof where he spent his childhood. Domus Orsoni, located in the Cannaregio district of Venice, has been created to welcome guests in an elegant mosaic environment. Orsoni has created the Masters in Mosaics course as the culmination of his desire to "spread the divine art of mosaics."

▲ **WHITE AND GOLD BATHROOM**
Orsoni white smalti, 24 k gold tesserae
Photo credit: Norbert Heyl

▸ **WHITE AND GOLD BATHROOM (DETAIL)**
Orsoni white smalti, 24 k gold tesserae
Photo credit: Norbert Heyl

Domus Orsoni allows guests to sleep nestled in beds with mosaic headboards. Nightstands and tables are graced with Orsoni smalti, and bathrooms are enhanced with various proportions of glass, marble, and wood. Each room has been designed by a notable Italian artist or architect, reflecting the artist's innovative sensibility interpreted in mosaic. In a departure from his creation of fine art, Orsoni designed one of the head-boards and two of the bathrooms. His diptych headboard is realized in black and 24 k gold smalti. The images derive from his reaction to September 11, 2001, and are dedicated to the memory of this cataclysmic event. The adjoining bathroom is a paradox. Intentionally minimal, with contrasting waves of white and 24 k gold, it is a precious rendition of the Adriatic Sea, which feeds the Venetian lagoon.

▲ **BEDROOM FURNITURE**
Mosaic design by Lucio Orsoni
Orsoni black smalti, 24 k gold tesserae, copper gold tesserae
Photo credit: Arnaldo Dal Bosco

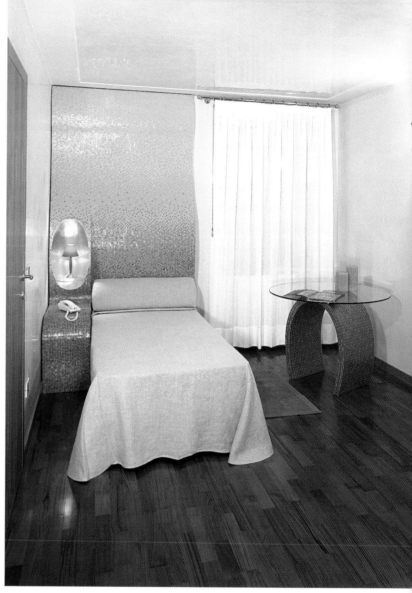

BEDROOM
Mosaic design by Marco Nereo Rotelli
Orsoni white smalti, 24 k gold tesserae
Photo credit: Arnaldo Dal Bosco

BEDROOM
Mosaic design by architect Carla Bratelli
Orsoni smalti (headboard), TREND glass mosaic
(nightstand)
Photo credit: Arnaldo Dal Bosco

BEDROOM
Mosaic design by architect Fabio Rotella
Orsoni 24 k gold tesserae, turquoise tesserae, mirror
Photo credit: Arnaldo Dal Bosco

▲ BLACK BATHROOM
Orsoni smalti, 24 k turquoise gold tesserae,
black glass tile
Photo credit: Norbert Heyl

The second bathroom created by Orsoni is unique in that the central mosaic is figurative—a woman ensconced against a field of black tile. His intention was to create a window to allow the viewer a glimpse outside. Like a '70s icon, the woman is liberated, without modesty, caught in a "particular moment of freedom." The juxtaposition of 24 k turquoise gold tesserae against the opaque glass of the woman creates a three-dimensional appearance. The woman stands almost within reach, just outside the window bars that protect her. Domus Orsoni is Orsoni's gift to the world. It represents his "goal of sharing and transferring to others the emotions I feel every day within the walls of the Orsoni factory"—historic walls that are a testament to the noble Venetian history of mosaics.

▲ HAT (DETAIL)
Italian vitreous glass
Photo credit: Serge Hack

▸ ENTRANCE TO SKYLAB
Ceramic, 24 k gold smalti
10' x 12' (3 x 3.6 m)
Photo credit: Serge Hack

laurel skye

IT STARTED WITH A TOASTER. Seven years ago, Laurel Skye was experiencing a life full of anguish: three marriages that didn't work, the death of a child, bad scars from a fire, a bout with cancer, the care of a mother with Alzheimer's disease, and bankruptcy. Then, a local bagel shop had a toaster contest. Skye tiled a toaster and won first prize. Winning the toaster contest resulted in an epiphany. Tiling saved her life.

One project led to the next, and Skye became the Pied Piper of Mosaic in the small northern California community of Arcata. Her turn-of-the-century home became a laboratory for her endless creations. No surface or implement escaped her hand. Instruments take on the glowing colors of Italian smalti. Hats that were once supple have become stiff with vitreous glass. Reflective Oriental carpets appeared underfoot. Mosaic clocks stand indifferent to night or day. Mosaic altars receive meditations and offer solace.

Not content to work incessantly on her own projects, Skye chose to share her passion by teaching at Skylab (her mosaic workshop). She tells her students, "I teach philosophy, but I'll throw mosaics in the cracks as we go along." Lest her students or any member of the community want for supplies, Skye decided to distribute mosaic materials from a wide variety of international sources.

▲ CARPET (DETAIL)
Italian and Mexican vitreous glass, ceramic
9' x 3' (2.9 x .9 m)
Photo credit: Serge Hack

◀ GUITAR (DETAIL)
Stained glass, Italian metallic glass, broken china
Photo credit: Serge Hack

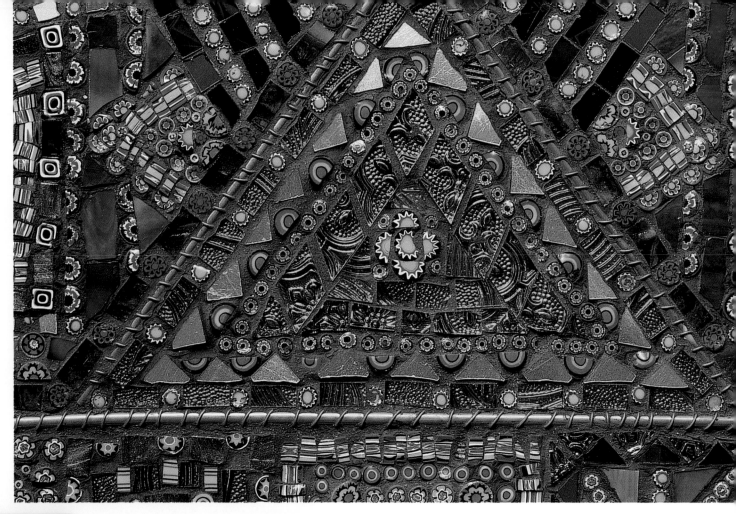

▲ MIRROR (DETAIL)
Vitreous and stained glass, gold smalti, mille fiori, copper tuber, ornate glass from Argentina
28" x 18" x 2" (71 x 46 x 5 cm)
Photo credit: Mark Lufkin

◄ CRUTCH (DETAIL)
Italian vitreous glass, ceramic and porcelain flowers
Photo credit: Serge Hack

▶ INDONESIAN BEDROOM
Photo credit: Mark Lufkin

In her home, Skye has created an Indonesian bedroom, referring to it as her "spare" bedroom; however, it is anything but. The room contains an altar for her mother, surrounded by crutches encrusted with flowers, which signify a South American tradition of "throw away your crutches and be healed." The master bathroom is a Turkish delight, a place to languish and luxuriate. An intricately mosaicked Buddha watches over the garden, an exercise that for Skye became "more spiritual journey than artistic endeavor."

▲ BUDDHA
Vitreous Italian metallic glass, gold smalti, ceramic
28" x 14" x 8" (71 x 36 x 20 cm)
Photo credit: Mark Lufkin

◀ BATHROOM
Italian and Mexican ceramic
Photo credit: Mark Lufkin

▼ BATHROOM (WALL DETAIL)
Photo credit: Mark Lufkin

▸ COWASAKI (DETAIL)
Italian vitreous glass
12" x 18" x 6" (30 x 46 x 15 cm)
Photo credit: Serge Hack

▾ KITCHEN
Photo credit: Mark Lufkin

▸ DINING ROOM TABLE WITH FRUIT
AND CLOCKS
Italian and Mexican vitreous glass and ceramic
Photo credit: Serge Hack

The mosaic adventure that started with a toaster is one of celebration, sacred spaces, and abundant humor. The tiled fruit will never rot in the bowl; Cowasaki, the guardian cow, roams from room to room; and the unexpected always surprises the unwitting guest. The creation of mosaic is as necessary to Skye as breathing. It takes her "to that magical junction where time and timelessness intersect." It is in this space that her home, a "vortex of energy," exists.

▾ **CATHEDRAL ENTRANCE**
Talavera tiles, vitreous glass, ceramic tiles
Photo credit: Mark Lufkin

◂ **CATHEDRAL ALTAR (DETAIL)**
Glass, iridium from Ravenna, tapestry glass from Argentina
Photo credit: Mark Lufkin

robyn
spencer-crompton

ROBYN SPENCER-CROMPTON CAME TO MOSAIC through what she considers the "back door." An internationally exhibited quiltmaker and theatrical costume designer, she has found mosaics offer the physical manifestation of the mythological spirit that inspires her. She creates her densely realized garden sculpture to give voice to the "mysteries of life that have no other language."

Mother is the undeniable union of earth and fertility. Holding an infant, the truncated pregnant form is layered with the veins of refuse. Starting with organic debris, such as shells, wood, and bones, the sculpture becomes encrusted with the detritus of modern life—bullets, soda can tabs, broken glass, and money. *Mother* spins unhindered from an ancient oak tree, a testament to the perpetuity of creation despite disregard for our planet.

▲ **MOTHER**
Shells, bones, rocks, found objects, polystyrene base
76" x 30" x 30" (193 x 76 x 76 cm)

▶ **MOTHER: BREAST AND ARM (DETAIL)**

▼ **MOTHER: BACK VIEW (DETAIL)**

The masculine essence of nature is the purpose of *Green Man*. Purported to be a pagan image, Spencer-Crompton and her husband Peter Crompton have, together, created a sculpture that continues the tradition of this archetype. Historically, this is a reclusive figure, and Spencer-Crompton has used color and texture to camouflage her contemporary interpretation among the foliage of their lavish gardens. *Green Man* emerges from the garden's depths as a heroic offering to those perceptive enough to find him.

⬍ GREEN MAN
Glass, terra-cotta, polished stones
30" x 36" x 16" (76 x 91 x 41 cm)

▲ GREEN MAN: LEFT SIDE (DETAIL)

▶ FISH BOY
Recycled glass, art glass, shells, concrete
52" x 16" x 16" (132 x 41 x 41 cm)

Peter Crompton, a painter, sculptor, and theatrical set designer, first participated with Spencer-Crompton on *Fish Boy*. Peter sculpts the forms and then, together, they create a concrete surface strengthened with polymer fibers and additives. It is then up to Spencer-Crompton to clad the forms in mosaic materials, using glass and found objects. According to Spencer-Crompton, "it is the part I like best—where meaningful content and glistening surfaces join the elegance of form, creating something significant as well as beautiful." Just as *Fish Boy* is a collaboration between husband and wife, he is also a Greco-Roman prototype of a boy riding a dolphin; the two images so closely aligned that they appear as a single entity representing a harmonious ideal.

▾ FISH BOY: FACE (DETAIL)

▶ FISH BOY: TAIL AND FEET (DETAIL)

Dagger Woman emerges from the shadows of a plank of black walnut to inspire courage. This mythological warrior evokes the profound indigenous lucidity created by a woman's instinct. She is a fearless forest sprite, adorned with brass findings that create her armor. Spencer-Crompton's mosaic art defies categorization. Although it is decorative in implementation, it is functional in purpose. Her sculptures provoke the viewer to explore the "archaic inner knowledge that lies below the surface of our daily perception."

‹ **DAGGER WOMAN**
Black walnut, brass findings, nails, rods
72" x 21" x 6" (183 x 53 x 15 cm)

⬍ **DAGGER WOMAN: FACE (DETAIL)**

▲ **DAGGER WOMAN: STRING SKIRT (DETAIL)**

◂ GLASGOW PANEL BATH
ELLEN MARSHALL RESIDENCE
Hand-cut opaque and translucent stained-glass
tesserae, Murano iridescent glass, beach glass
140' (42 m) square
Photo credit: Gregory R. Staley

▸ GLASGOW PANEL BATH (DETAIL)
Photo credit: Gregory R. Staley

judy stone

HOW OFTEN IS IT that a whim can alter the course of a life? Judy Stone's occupation as a mosaic artist was launched on such a whim when she created the birdbath that instigated her career. Familiarizing herself with the bevy of materials that make up the mosaicist's palette, she cemented her artistic vision with the discovery of cut stained glass. The color choice with this medium is virtually unlimited, and the translucent and iridescent quality of the glass produce bejeweled surfaces. The laborious methodology of mosaic creation is an integral part of the process, because Stone accepts only one commission at a time, allowing her to focus completely on the unique sensibilities of each project.

Charles Rennie Mackintosh provided the motivation for a floor-to-ceiling tub surround in a custom-built Arts and Crafts–inspired home. Graphically reminiscent of the Glasgow School of Arts' main entrance, the geometric gridlike application of glass is punctuated by the stylized rose motif that Mackintosh imbued with a profound directive: the flower being to art what the green leaf is to life.

▲ **GLASGOW PANEL BATH (DETAIL)**
Photo credit: Gregory R. Staley

◄ **GLASGOW PANEL BATH (DETAIL)**
Photo credit: Gregory R. Staley

A vacation to Australia provided the stimulus for a kitchen back-splash soliloquy. The indigenous aboriginal shapes and forms that inhabit dream paintings now characterize a personal "walk-about." Fabricated in opaque and translucent stained-glass tesserae, the kitchen mosaic contributes an intimate ethnic ingredient to family meals.

▾ WALKABOUT BACKSPLASH (DETAIL)
Photo credit: Gregory R. Staley

⤵ WALKABOUT BACKSPLASH (DETAIL)
Photo credit: Gregory R. Staley

▶ FLAME THROWER FIREPLACE
JANICE AND LUCIUS JACKSON RESIDENCE
Hand-cut opaque and translucent stained-glass tesserae
4' x 5' x 6' fireplace surround (1 x 2 x 2 m)
5' x 18" hearth (2 m x 46 cm)
Photo credit: Gregory R. Staley

Working in glass has allowed Stone the freedom to manipulate the hand-cut pieces to create three-dimensional relief or turn a particularly difficult corner. The *Flame Thrower* fireplace is a brilliant amalgamation of complementary hues that achieve a mesmerizing combustion of reflection and depth. What was once an unsightly brick fireplace has now become the heart of an artistic home.

⬍ FLAME THROWER FIREPLACE (DETAIL)
Photo credit: Gregory R. Staley

▲ FLAME THROWER FIREPLACE (DETAIL)
Photo credit: Gregory R. Staley

▶ PYRAMID TABLE TOP (DETAIL)
Photo credit: Gregory R. Staley

And the birdbaths? They still exist. Mirroring the circulation of water, Stone adorns the stock garden sculpture with the stunning colors that inhabit her residential commissions. On the *Bluebird Bath*, Stone has "planted" a relief vine threading its way up the base of the sculpture, creating movement with glass. Mackintosh would approve of her inclusion of nature to create animation on an object devoid of mobility. He knew these endeavors made things "precious—more beautiful—more lasting than life."

▲ BLUEBIRD BATH
Hand-cut opaque and translucent stained-glass tesserae
27" x 18" x 18" (69 x 46 x 46 cm)
Photo credit: Gregory R. Stanley
Collection of Binnie Fry

craigie s. succop

A MOVE TO MARYLAND'S EASTERN SHORE in 1995 was the catalyst that unleashed Craigie Succop's passion for glass and sculptural mosaics. Organic forms and animals populate her world, featuring glass as both a medium and instigator. "I tend to concentrate on curves, lines, shapes, and textures, letting the glass ultimately tell me where it wants to go," she explains. Succop hand-cuts all the glass and hand-blends all her mortar colors, which adds depth to her installations.

A mosaicked wind vane situated on a piling is a constant reminder of nature's impact on the land that Succop occupies. Water continues as an important theme—her garden is home to two fountains: *The World*, a hollow fiberglass ball emblazoned with metallic and opaque glass, and the *Whale Lily Pond*, which appears to be a delightful wading pool enclosed by a friendly cetacean marine mammal.

Animals populate much of Succop's work—a gecko, a butterfly, and a turtle have all appeared, larger than life, and taken up residence on exterior walls. And lest her home feel inanimate compared to the menagerie of animals, Succop has supplied "eyebrows" in many of the rooms—an unconventional window treatment that adds expression, color, and texture to her interiors. The eponymous *Four Seasons* are reflected in an expansive 21-foot (6.4 m) mural running the length of her entire living room. Mosaic-enhanced tables, fireplace screens, and bathtubs have also become a part of her living environment, allowing her art to function as decorative furnishings.

⌃ WIND VANE
Metal and ceramic tile
3' x 3' (1 x 1 m)

▲ THE WORLD FOUNTAIN
Glass on a hollow fiberglass ball
5' (2 m) diameter
Photo credit: Richard Dorbin,
Paragon Light Photography

▸ WHALE LILY POND
Ceramic, glass, agates
22' x 10' (7 x 3 m)

▲ **ALATS THE GECKO**
Glass
8' x 4' (2 x 1m)

◄ **MO, THE MOSAIC TURTLE**
Glass, ceramic, agates, polished stones, mirror
5' x 3½' (2 x 1m)

▾ **BUTTERFLY (DETAIL)**
Glass, beads, mirror
5' x 4' (2 x 1m)

▸ **LIVING ROOM EYEBROW**
Glass
24" x 12" (61 x 30 cm)

▾ **KITCHEN EYEBROWS**
Glass
24" x 12" (61 x 30 cm)

▴ **THE FOUR SEASONS**
Glass on glass, lit from behind.
18' x 2½' (5 x 1 m).
Photo credit: Richard Dorbin, Paragon
Light Photography

▸ **FIREPLACE SCREEN AND INFINITY
WALL PANEL**
Glass, agates, copper.
3' x 5' (1 x 2 m) (wall panel).
Photo credit: Richard Dorbin, Paragon
Light Photography.

Succop has immortalized her own features by casting her face and adding a mosaic likeness to a routed-out cypress knee. Fondly referred to as the *Keeper of the Cove*, this garden sculpture is evocative and resourceful and enhances the beauty of what nature has already initiated.

▲ PHOENIX PORTICO—PRIVATE RESIDENCE
Tumbled limestone, marble, seashells, malachite,
lapis lazuli, onyx, jasper, ceramic tile, glass, gold, agate
200' (61 m) square

karen thompson

Karen Thompson has what most artists only dream about—a benefactor. Since 1997, Thompson has been creating mosaics for her patron's two residences. Over the years, a trust has developed that allows her the freedom to create without limitation. She is able to explore new processes and materials under the auspices of her patron, who is dedicated to nurturing artists. Thompson relishes this freedom and uses an exotic palette of materials, including semiprecious stones, ancient fossils, marble, granite, and limestone accented with beads, gemstones, and seashells.

Together with Julie Goodson-Lawes, a painter and muralist, and her assistant Mary Grae, Thompson has achieved a visual testament to the integration of art, architecture, and fantasy. A groin ceiling welcomes guests to the Phoenix residence portico, where stylized insects are set into a limestone floor. The French doors of the trompe l'oeil wall panel lead to a marble stairway and glass observatory crowned with a gold dome. A luminous peacock beckons, tail feathers spilling onto the floor and merging the wall mosaic and pavement in one fluid motion.

▲ PHOENIX PORTICO: WALL PANEL (DETAIL)

◄ PHOENIX PORTICO: PAVEMENT (DETAIL)
Photo credit: David Peterson

▼ PHOENIX PORTICO: PEACOCK (DETAIL)

▲ SAN FRANCISCO PARLOR PANELS
PRIVATE RESIDENCE
Marble, granite, glass, semiprecious stones, ancient
fossils, seashells, beads, ribbons, dichroic glass,
hand-dyed paper, and gemstones
115' (34.8 m) square
Photo credit: David Peterson

▶ SAN FRANCISCO PARLOR PANEL (DETAIL)
Photo credit: David Peterson

In the San Francisco residence, Thompson has translated the art of the Victorian painter Sir Lawrence Alma-Tadema into a series of stunning panels for the formal parlor. Still lifes are replete with effusive bouquets, and elaborate terraces are adorned with women in repose. Intricate details capture a moment in time as pomegranate juice is spilled by a determined bird, candlelight flickers, and books are left open to the last page read. A finch holds a banner proclaiming in Latin, "vita sine artis mors est" — life without art is death.

Thompson's glass-lamination process allows the use of fragile materials, protecting them with layers of glass. In the formal parlor, grass is created by arranging various hues of green bugle beads between clear and stained glass. Hand-dyed paper from India, stitched in gold thread, was used to form a woman's dress, which was then laminated with clear glass.

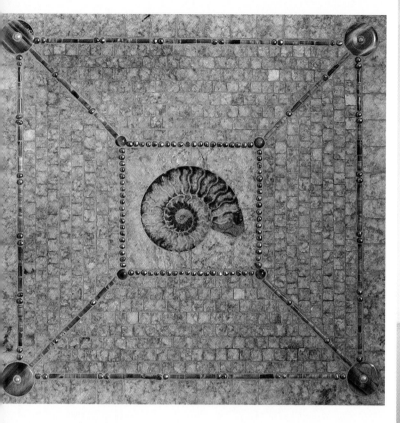

▲ SAN FRANCISCO PARLOR PANEL: FOSSIL
(DETAIL)
Photo credit: David Peterson

▸ SAN FRANCISCO PARLOR PANELS
Photo credit: David Peterson

▸ SAN FRANCISCO PARLOR PANELS
PRIVATE RESIDENCE
Marble, granite, stained glass, semiprecious stone,
seashell, beads, ribbon, paper
45" x 52" (114 x 132 cm)
Photo credit: Todd Pickering

▲ FIREPLACE SURROUND—PRIVATE
RESIDENCE
Glass, marbles
30' (9.1 m) square
Photo credit: Rebecca Ford

◄ MOROCCAN-INSPIRED GARDEN FOUNTAIN
PRIVATE RESIDENCE
Ceramic tile, glass, stained concrete
4' x 4' x 12" (1.2 m x 1.2 m x 30 cm)
Photo credit: Jeremy Templer

◄ KITCHEN—PRIVATE RESIDENCE
50' (15 m) square
Photo credit: Russell MacMasters

Thompson is self-taught, discovering mosaics in the process of restoring her home. Since 1987, her life amid broken tile has led to a vast array of custom commissions for private homes and gardens, restaurants, public spaces, religious institutions, and retail stores. The choice of materials is of particular importance to her. "I want my mosaics to seem like they really belong in their environment. Certain materials just seem to fit and complement the feel of a place, rather than being imposed or forced." Guided by instinct, Thompson integrates an elegant presence in mosaic.

laurel true

IT IS NOT EVERY EIGHT-YEAR-OLD that can see into the future and know with true conviction that she will become an artist. Then again, it is not every artist who is also a fortune-teller. Laurel True is a peripatetic visionary, exploring cultures as diverse as those of Senegal, Africa, and Ravenna, Italy, to realize her childhood ambition.

An adored teacher, True divides her time between private and public commissions by teaching in various parts of the world. Her energy is contagious, and her quest for experimentation and knowledge confirm her identity as a perpetual student. Experimenting with new techniques, pushing the physical boundaries of her mosaic materials, and creating an aesthetic language that communicates her intention—whether in West Africa or West Oakland—True has enlivened neighborhoods with scenic maps that exalt diversity and the colorful citizenry that inhabit urban settings.

▲ IYAKERE'S DOOR
Ceramic tile, glass, shells, beads, mirror, mixed-media mosaic
32" x 78" (81 x 198 cm)
Photo credit: David Meiland

▼ IYAKERE'S DOOR (DETAIL)
Photo credit: David Meiland

▶ SPIRAL KITCHEN FOR STRAWBALE HOUSE
Ceramic tile, slate
30' (9 m) square
Photo credit: David Meiland

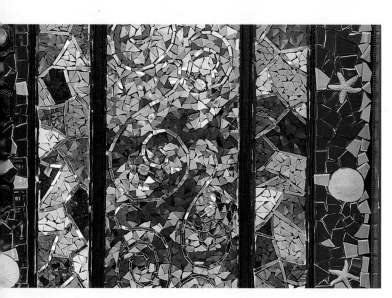

▲ UNDERWATER BATHROOM MURAL
PRIVATE RESIDENCE
Glass, gems, mirror
62" x 42" (157 x 107 cm)
Photo credit: David Meiland

◄ UNDERWATER BATHROOM MURAL
(DETAIL)
Photo credit: David Meiland
Production assistance by Tammy Lee for
True Mosaic Studio

▲ VELOCITY CIRCUS MUSEUM CIRCLE BAR
Glass, mirror
85' x 45" x 21" (21.6 m x 114 x 53 cm)
Photo credit: David Bowman

▸ VELOCITY CIRCUS MUSEUM:
ELEMENTS DOOR
Glass and mirror mosaic
32" x 78" (81 x 198 cm)
Photo credit: David Bowman

◄ VELOCITY CIRCUS MUSEUM: DOUBLE
HELIX MURAL (DETAIL)
Glass, mirror, antique gems
22" x 60" (56 cm x 152 cm)
Photo credit: David Meiland

The synergy that True creates, using her art as a device to create ornamentation, has captured the cosmos of Gregangelo Herrera. Impresario and owner of the Velocity Circus, Herrera and True have worked together to transform his San Francisco home into a museum of dreams, both sacred and profane. True's interpretation of universal themes has infiltrated the residence; the result is a flamboyant and deeply personal environment.

Delicate dichroic glass dragonflies hum against black tile; the planets spin on a glowing backsplash. Caffeine is redundant as one enters the breakfast area that replicates dawn—opalescent swimming-pool tile and jewel-toned mirrored glass jolt you into daily wakefulness. The themes are mystical; the solar system takes its place among the elements of earth, air, fire, and water. Infinity is perpetuated in mirrored reflections. Client and artist speak a privileged language of shared vision. Design decisions evolve from a honed telepathy filled with riotous color, humor, and blatant disregard for traditional mosaic precedents.

◄ VELOCITY CIRCUS MUSEUM:
CANDY COUNTER
Glass and mirror mosaic
7' x 34" x 18" (2 m x 86 cm x 46 cm)
Photo credit: David Meiland

▼ VELOCITY CIRCUS MUSEUM:
ELEMENTS DOOR (DETAIL)
Photo credit: David Bowman

▶ **VELOCITY CIRCUS MUSEUM DINING ROOM**
Glass, mirror, swimming-pool tile, mixed-media mosaic
9' x 10' (2.7 x 3 m)
Photo credit: David Bowman

◀ **VELOCITY CIRCUS MUSEUM KITCHEN: PLANETARY CONSTELLATION MURAL**
Glass, mirror, antique gems, mixed-media mosaic
22" x 15' (56 cm x 5 m)
Photo credit: David Bowman

◀ **VELOCITY CIRCUS MUSEUM DRAGONFLY CART (DETAIL)**
Yukari Kato for True Mosaics Studio. Glass, mirror, dichroic glass.
30" x 12" (76 x 30 cm).
Photo credit: David Bowman

▶ **VELOCITY CIRCUS MUSEUM KITCHEN: PLANETARY CONSTELLATION MURAL (DETAIL)**
Photo credit: David Meiland

▲ TWIN THRONES (DETAIL)
Commissioned by Friends of Duboce Park
Neighborhood Association
Ceramic tile, glass gems, mirror, concrete
55' (16 m) square

◀ CREATIVITY ARCHWAY
NUNGUA, GHANA, AFRICA
In partnership with the Cross Cultural
Collaborative, Inc.
Ceramic tile, beach pebbles, shells, mirror
12' x 18' (4 x 5 m)

As a performer, Herrera has astonished audiences as a secular whirling dervish. True's commissions and teaching assignments take her throughout the United States, venturing as far as Africa, where she spends summers teaching and creating community mosaics in Ghana. In her spare time, she runs marathons. Perhaps it is their desire for motion that has united these two souls, leading them to concoct dazzling spaces and inspiring their fertile minds.

gallery

This gallery is divided into two sections, Private Spaces and Public Spaces. Within each section are international representations of mosaic art that reflects an integration of art and lifestyle. Private spaces are the environments in which our daily lives unfold. Each of the four sections—Bathing, Eating, Living, and Relaxing—contains examples of living spaces that have been personalized by mosaic art. A love of pugs provides the inspiration for a patio medallion, a bathroom reflects a passion for fluid dynamics imagery, and a bedroom vanity becomes a fantasy in Limoges china.

In the Public section of the Gallery, the mosaic art shown is available to be experienced by everyone and has often become the solution for an ecological or community concern. Healing and Learning display mosaic applications where there is often civic, student, and restorative pride. They represent the curative power of mosaics in schools, hospitals, libraries, shelters, and even an art gallery that greets visitors with the adage, "Life is an art not a science."

In the Dining and Resting sections, commercial applications are presented in restaurants and hotels. A coffee bar in Ravenna, Italy, is lavished with mosaic treatments—walls, floors, bar, and tables glimmer with metallic surfaces and opulent colors. Hotels in Mexico, New Zealand, and Santa Fe, New Mexico, reflect the unique artistry of the owners and are all enchanted lodgings where guests can inhabit a mosaic experience, savoring a glimpse of how it feels to live with mosaics, if only temporarily.

private spaces :

bathing

ahmed agrama

TOILET PAPER HOLDER
Handmade ceramic tile
10" x 10" x 6" (25 x 25 x 15 cm)

eating

louis g. weiner and cindy d. jones

RUG-INSPIRED DINING TABLE
Italian vitreous glass
30" x 4' x 6' (76 cm x 1.2 m x 1.8 m)

living

sarit pilz granit

ARMCHAIR
Golden blue-glass tesserae, mirror tesserae in gold, hand-painted ceramic tesserae, dark gray grout, wooden frame
35½" x 31½" x 27½" (90 x 80 x 70 cm)
Photo credit: Shay Adam

relaxing

sherry mccall

MERMAID BENCH
Bisazza's Metron, concrete board, latex-enhanced thinset.
20" x 40" x 19" (51 cm x 40 cm x 19 cm)
Photo credit: Dennis O'Kain

twyla arthur

▲ ARTIST'S BATHROOM WITH MOSAIC
MIRROR AND SHELF
Travertine mosaic with shells and rocks
110' (33.3 m) square
Photo credit: Ansen Seale

haruo nakabayashi

▼ BATHROOM
Marble and glass mosaic tile
8¼' x 8¼' (2.5 m x 2.5 m)
Photo credit: Hidenori Hara

robert stout and
stephanie jurs

▲ FLOW MOTION, DERIVED FROM FLUID
DYNAMICS IMAGERY
Private residence
Interior design by Deborah Michie
Solid-body porcelain tiles, gold Venetian tile
65' (6.04 m) square
Photo credit: Deborah Michie Interior Design

▼ FLOW MOTION, DERIVED FROM FLUID
DYNAMICS IMAGERY (DETAIL)
Private residence
Interior design by Deborah Michie
Solid-body porcelain tiles, gold Venetian tile
Photo credit: Deborah Michie Interior Design

lillian sizemore

▲ WOMEN'S REST ROOM
Brand New Media, ad agency
McIntyre ceramic tile, Malibu tile, colored grout,
mirror on wood
48" (122 cm) diameter
Photo credit: Mona Kuhn, styled by Lillian Sizemore

▼ WOMEN'S REST ROOM (FLOOR DETAIL)
Photo credit: Mona Kuhn

filippo tazzari

▲ LAVACRUM
Interior design by Ivana Porfiri Studio
Glass, gold, quartz, amethyst
6' x 14' (185 x 420 cm)
Photo credit: Andrea Ferrari

◄ PRINCIPIUM
Interior design by Ivana Porfiri Studio
Glass, gold, quartz, amethyst
6' x 13' 4" (183 x 400 cm)
Photo credit: Andrea Ferrari

irina charny

◂ GUEST BATHROOM WALLS AND MIRROR
Ceramic tile
75' (23 m) square
Photo credit: Ben Charny

▾ GUEST BATHROOM CORNER (DETAIL)
Photo credit: Ben Charny

deb carlson wight

◄ SHOWER WAVES: "FREDDO"
Travertine, marble, glass.
14' (4 m) square.
Photo credit: Vernon Wentz

▼ SHOWER WAVES: "FREDDO" (DETAIL)
Photo credit: Vernon Wentz

julia di biasi

▸ MOSAIC BATH
Handmade and hand-painted ceramic tiles; glass
gems from Spain, Italy, India, and Mexico; plates
and found objects from Thailand, Singapore, India,
and Italy
36' (11 m) square
Photo credit: Warren Cipa

◄ MOSAIC BATH (DETAIL)
Photo credit: Warren Cipa

irina charny

▸ **FLOWER BACKSPLASH**
Vitreous glass, unglazed porcelain, stained glass,
gold, pebbles, beads
38" x 20" (97 x 51 cm)
Photo credit: Ben Charny

▴ **FLOWER BACKSPLASH (DETAIL)**
Photo credit: Ben Charny

cheryl evans

▸ **KALEIDOSCOPE (PORTABLE KITCHEN ISLAND TOPPER)**
Art glass on wood
4" x 24" x 48" (10 x 61 x 122 cm)
Photo credit: Howard Rosenzweig

▾ **KALEIDOSCOPE (DETAIL)**
Photo credit: Howard Rosenzweig

gina hubler and jackie gran

▸ CHICKEN FAMILIA
Jackie Gran residence
Smalti, marble, gold
60" x 12" (152 x 30 cm)

▲ CHICKEN FAMILIA (DETAIL)

natsu kaji

▲ **KITCHEN**
Ceramic tile, terra-cotta tile, marble
5' 9" x 11' 9" x 8' 9" (1.8 x 3.6 x 2.7 m)
Photo credit: Mariko Nakagawa

▶ **KITCHEN WALL (DETAIL)**
Ceramic tile
Photo credit: Mariko Nakagawa

deb carlson wight

▼ **TALAVERA ARCHES**
Travertine, marble, glass, and talavera
30' (9 m) square
Photo credit: Joel Spring

candace bahouth

◂ **FRENCH MOSAIC TAPESTRY CHAIR**
Porcelain tesserae, wood, glue, grout
54" x 31" x 25" (137 x 79 x 64 cm)

▴ **FRENCH MOSAIC TAPESTRY CHAIR
(DETAIL)**
Porcelain tesserae, wood, glue, grout

mindy simbrat

▸ **LIMOGES DAYDREAM**
Vintage china, porcelain flowers.
59" x 40" x 18" (150 x 102 x 46 cm)
Photo credit: Kevin Rouse

joanne berke

▾ LIVING ROOM WITH MOSAICKED FIRE-
PLACE, OTTOMAN, AND SCULPTURES
Ceramic, glass and mirror tile
Photo credit: Vaughn Hutchinson

◂ SCULPTURE AND FIREPLACE (DETAIL)
Ceramic tile, glass tile, mirror tile
Photo credit: Vaughn Hutchinson

enzo tinarelli

▴ CARRARA CURTAIN
Marble, glass tiles, gold
55" x 25 ½" x 51" (140 x 65 x 20 cm)
Photo credit: Fabio Amerio

▸ GENETIC CARPET
Marble, enamel, gold, turquoise
90 ½" x 51" (230 x 130 cm)
Photo credit: Fabio Amerio

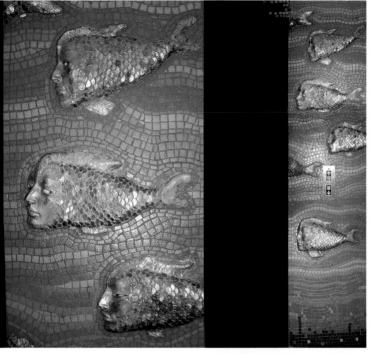

claudia nagy

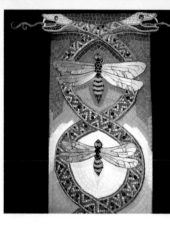

‣ FRAUFISH
One of seven hall murals commissioned by the Red Square Apartment Building, New York, New York
Venetian glass smalti, pennies, cement cast with one-cent scales, copper leaf, doll's eyes
93" x 34" (236 x 86 cm).
Photo credit: Craig Zipper

▴ FRAUFISH (DETAIL)
Photo credit: Craig Zipper

‣ TWO SNAKES AND TWO BEES (DETAIL)
Venetian glass mosaic, wood, aluminum, glass eyes
93" x 34" (236 x 86 cm)
Photo credit: Craig Zipper

george fishman

▴ FLAMING FIREPLACE
Glass smalti, stone, quarry tile.
60" x 48" x 24" (152 x 122 x 61 cm)

‣ FLAMING FIREPLACE (DETAIL)

laurie mika

▾ LIT LAMP
Lamp, acrylic paint, smalti, micromosaics,
gold chips, jewelry, beads
30" x 7" x 7" (76 x 18 x 18 cm)
Photo credit: Araceli Galindo

karen ami

▴ GARDEN OF TEMPTATION: FIREPLACE
Clay, glazes, vitreous glass tile, smalti, glass,
handmade clay tiles
10' x 5' 6" (3 x 2 m)
Photo credit: Edward Daniel Photography

⛇ GARDEN OF TEMPTATION: ADAM (DETAIL)
Photo credit: Edward Daniel Photography

▸ GARDEN OF TEMPTATION: SNAKE (DETAIL)
Photo credit: Edward Daniel Photography

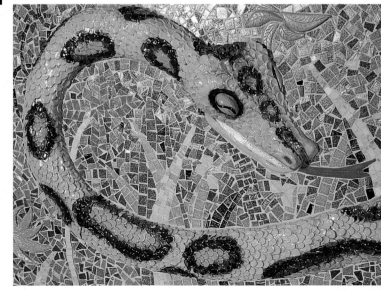

carol bevilacqua

▲ BOOMERANG WALL FAÇADE
Scratchcoat cement form over wood and wire
designed into boomerang shape
Handmade incised and pressed diamond, triangle,
and flower ceramic tiles incorporated with field tiles
15' x 4'3" (4.5 m x 1 m x 91 cm)

▶ BOOMERANG WALL FAÇADE (DETAIL)

sonia king

◀ LEAF FLOOR
Glass and ceramic
66' (20 m) square
Photo credit: Sheila Cunningham

▶ LEAF FLOOR (DETAIL)
Photo credit: Sheila Cunningham

Mosaic exists in a place somewhere between fine art, craft, and manufacturing. It is a manmade art in which a search for expression is intertwined with the need to resolve functional problems: a manmade art where the delicacy of light and heaviness of the material coexist, where the immediacy of the viewer's perception is countered by the slow meticulousness of the artist's execution. —LUCIANA NOTTURNI

luciana notturni

▲ **LAMPADA (LAMP)**
Designer: Alessandro Mendini, installed in a permanent exhibition in Holland
Venetian smalti
110½" x 23½" (280 x 60 cm) diameter
Photo credit: Enzo Pezzi

▶ **DINING TABLETOP**
Architect: Pier Carlo Bontempi
Private collection
Marble with Venetian smalti mosaic insert
47" (120 cm) diameter
Photo credit: Enzo Pezzi

◀ **DINING TABLETOP INSERT (DETAIL)**
Photo credit: Enzo Pezzi

private spaces : relaxing

xuan my ho

▲ HOROSCOPE BIRDBATH
China, rocks, twelve horoscope animals,
glass, marbles
27" x 23" (69 x 58 cm)
Photo credit: Minh Hong

⬧ HOROSCOPE BIRDBATH BASE (DETAIL)
Photo credit: Minh Hong

haruo nakabayashi

▲ WAVE
Granitos, marble
6' x 17' (2 x 5 m)
Photo credit: Hidenori Hara

nancy wittels

▸ **PUGS ON THE PATIO**
Porcelain, stoneware ceramics
48" (122 cm) diameter medallion

▾ **PUGS ON THE PATIO (DETAIL)**

pattie grey

◂ **STUFFED SHIRT**
Mannequin, dishes, tile, glue, grout
20" x 17" x 10" (51 x 43 x 25 cm)

linda beaumont

▸ **SEE YOU THERE: COMPOSTING PRIVY**
Seen in winter on the Badanes estate, Prickly
Mountain, Vermont
Mirror, ceramic plates, found objects
10' x 12' x 5' (3 x 4 x 2 m)
Photo credit: Ann Schaller

ilana shafir

▸ HANGING MOSAIC IN THE GARDEN
Marble, industrial tiles, ceramics, Murano glass,
gold tesserae
16" x 26" x 1½" (40 x 68 x 4 cm)
Photo credit: Giora Shafir

▾ HANGING MOSAIC IN THE GARDEN
(DETAIL)
Photo credit: Giora Shafir

julie charles

◂ AMERICAN TRIO
Regulation bowling pins, broken china, tile,
found objects
16" x 5" x 5" (41 x 13 x 13 cm)

gordan mandich

▲ SEASONS FOUNTAIN
Smalti, gold, silver, ceramic, vitreous glass
53" x 49" x 21½" (135 x 125 x 55 cm)

▶ FLORA FOUNTAIN
Ceramic tiles.
27 ½" x 63" (70 x 160 cm)

linda prince

◀ THE SHOE
Pottery mold, vintage and antique china, black grout
9" x 5" (23 x 13 cm)

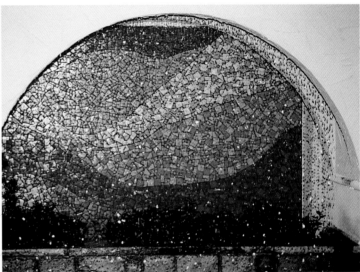

tracy gravier bell and robin oldham franklin

◀ RIBBON MURAL
Broken glass
24" x 6' (61 cm x 2 m)

▲ RIBBON MURAL (DETAIL)
Broken glass

louis g. weiner and cindy d. jones

▸ POOLSIDE MURAL
Vitreous glass tile
4' x 14' (1 x 4 m)

▲ POOLSIDE MURAL (DETAIL)

steven vella

▲ SAVAGE GARDEN: POOL MOSAIC WITH
WATER FEATURE
Inspired by Henri Rousseau's *Snake Charmer*
Private residence, Bondi, Australia
Vitreous glass
9' 9" x 10' 6" (3 x 3.2 m)

◂ UNTITLED SCULPTURE
Vitreous glass on carved Hebel block
23½" x 13½" x 13½" (60 x 35 x 35 cm)

tina amidon

▲ **FOUNTAIN OF FLOWERS**
Drag bucket, steel discs, inverted 1900 lamp base, water handle, glass, gold smalti, china, beach glass
6' x 36" x 2" (2 m x 91 cm x 5 cm)
Photo credit: George Post

◄ **FOUNTAIN OF FLOWERS (DETAIL)**

carol bevilacqua

▼ **FLOWER POWER SAINT STONE**
Hand-painted, molded, glazed ceramic and porcelain tiles, designed and constructed on wire and cement base.
15" x 17" x 15" (38 x 43 x 38 cm)

▶ **FLOWER POWER SAINT STONE (DETAIL)**

bea pereira

‣ **NYMPHÉAS FOUNTAIN (DETAIL)**
Photo credit: Rosângela Kusma Gasparin

▾ **NYMPHÉAS FOUNTAIN**
Inspired by Claude Monet
Brick, cement, glazed ceramic tile, vitreous
glass, porcelain
24" x 12' x 14' (61 cm x 4 m x 4 m)
Photo credit: Rosângela Kusma Gasparin

gina dominguez

▴ **SUNFLOWER: OUTDOOR GARDEN
BIRDBATH**
Cement base adorned with ceramic tile
30" x 24" (76 x 61 cm)
Photo credit: Milton Cheng

‣ **SUNFLOWER: OUTDOOR GARDEN
BIRDBATH (DETAIL)**
Photo credit: Milton Cheng

lynn adamo

▸ **TEATIME FOR THE BIRDS ON A RAINY DAY**
Handbuilt ceramic form, mixed-media mosaic
(ceramic and glass)
6' x 22" (2 m x 56 cm) diameter

◂ **TEATIME FOR THE BIRDS ON A RAINY DAY
(DETAIL)**

john t. unger

▴ **ACROBAT FENCE**
Steel, porcelain tile mosaic
48" x 120" x 2" (122 x 305 x 5 cm)
Photo credit: Jeanne Hannah

◂ **ACROBAT FENCE (DETAIL)**
Photo credit: Jeanne Hannah

rosângela k. gasparin

▸ **SYMBOLS OF PARANÁ: A PITCHER USING
TWO MOTIFS—THE ARAUCARIA PINE AND
THE GRALHA AZUL BIRD, BOTH SYMBOLS
OF THE SOUTHERN BRAZIL REGION.**
Terra-cotta, glazed ceramic tiles, vitreous glass tiles,
porcelain tiles, colored glass, agate pebbles,
Brazilian stones, and pine (araucaria) seed shell
38" x 27" x 15" (97 x 69 x 38 cm)

public spaces :

dining

daniela caravita

BAR VERDERAME (DETAIL)
Ravenna, Italy
Project Architect: Luca Piccirillo
Glass, vitreous paste, murrine, gold glass

healing

sonia king

NATURE WALL (DETAIL)
Children's Hospital of Dallas
Glass, ceramic, dichroic gems, glass fusions
Photo credit: Scott Williams

learning

mary ann moore, professor
Assisted by students at Oklahoma City Community College

BATTLE OF HONEY SPRINGS
Originally designed by the late professor Paul Ringler
Porcelain, commercial tiles
12' x 32' (4 x 10 m)

resting

sylvia seret

SUITE 22, INN OF FIVE GRACES
Santa Fe, New Mexico
Broken talavera field tile, patterned tile, broken Jaipur
pottery, clipped pots cut in half
8' x 5' (2.4 x 1.5 m)
Photo credit: Scot Zimmerman

public spaces : dining

kii toyoharu

◂ BAKERY FLOOR MOSAIC
Marble
2' (.5 m) square

santiago rodriguez

▸ METRO TULIP PILLARS
San Francisco, California
Glass tile, salvaged ship masts
10' x 20" (3 m x 51 cm)
Photo credit: Alexander Warnow Photography

◂ METRO TULIP PILLAR (DETAIL)
San Francisco, California
Photo credit: Alexander Warnow Photography

allison goldenstein and lesley provenzano

▲ MOHEGAN SUN CASINO SUNBURST CAFÉ
Uncasville, Connecticut
Architect: David Rockwell
Stained glass
50' x 20' (15 x 6 m)
Photo credit: Gary Goldenstein

▶ LOCO NOCHE: DANCING LADIES
New York, New York
Stained glass, mirror, glass nuggets
10' x 14' (3 x 4 m)
Photo credit: Gary Goldenstein

akomena

⌃ **PINETTA**
Milano, Marittima, Italy
Architect: Marco Lucchi
Hand-cut white Bianco Trani marble, hand-cut black
Nero Marquina marble

▸ **PINETTA (DETAIL)**

▴ **BY PASS**
Geneva, Switzerland
Architect: Marco Lucchi
Hand-cut white Bianco Trani marble, hand-cut black
Nero Marquina marble

◂ **BY PASS (DETAIL)**

claudia tedeschi and
ermanno carbonara

▸ BAR VERDERAME: TABLE (DETAIL)
Ravenna, Italy
Architect: Luca Piccirillo
Glass, vitreous paste, murrine, gold glass,
stones, shells

⬍ BAR VERDERAME: TABLE (DETAIL)

▴ BAR VERDERAME: TABLE (DETAIL)

daniela caravita, claudia tedeschi, and ermanno carbonara

▴ Bar Verderame: Table and floor (detail)

daniela caravita

▾ BAR VERDERAME: FLOOR (DETAIL)
Ravenna, Italy
Architect: Luca Piccirillo
Glass, vitreous paste, murrine, gold glass

◂ BAR VERDERAME: BAR (DETAIL)

public spaces : healing

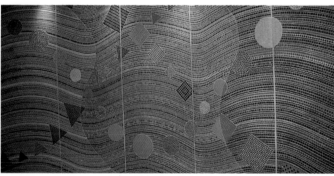

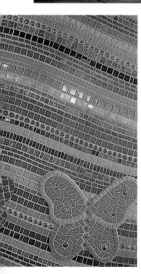

sonia king

⭷ NATURE WALL
Children's Medical Center of Dallas
Glass, ceramic, dichroic gems, glass fusions
8' x 17' (2.4 x 5.1 m)
Photo credit: Scott Williams

◂ NATURE WALL (DETAIL)
Photo credit: Scott Williams

⭷ SHAPES WALL
Children's Medical Center of Dallas
Glass, ceramic, dichroic gems, glass fusions

▸ SHAPES WALL (DETAIL)

susan wink

⌃ LEAF BENCH
This bench was created for the Assurance Home,
a safe house for abused and neglected teenagers.
All the tiles covering the bench were created by
residents and staff working together with the artist
Susan Wink.
Cement, handmade tile, grout
48" x 10' x 40" (122 cm x 3 m x 102 cm)

⌃ LEAF BENCH (DETAIL)

robert stout and
stephanie jurs

▸ FOUNTAIN FOR YOUTH
Created for a facility of disturbed teenagers, the
intention of the fountain was to create a calming
and relaxing place for the troubled young residents.
The exterior is a quattro-foil design.
Solid-body porcelain tiles, glass smalti, Italian
porcelain, granite overflow spouts, granite tiles
21' (6.4 m) diameter

⌃ FOUNTAIN FOR YOUTH (DETAIL)

debby hagar

▸ **BENNETT ART GALLERY: DOOR SURROUND "LIFE IS ART NOT A SCIENCE"**
Handmade tile, mosaic
104" x 102" x 2" (264 x 259 x 5 cm)
Photo credit: Charles Brooks

▸ **BENNETT ART GALLERY: DOOR SURROUND**
Photo credit: Charles Brooks

betty rosen ziff and the residents of refugee safe haven

▸ **7 WONDERS OF THEIR WORLD**
Cement tiles, adhesive, Wonderboard, black grout
60" x 36" (152 x 91 cm)
This mural was designed and fabricated with the residents of Refugee Safe Haven, the only shelter for refugees in Los Angeles, as part of an Artist in Residence grant received from the Los Angeles Cultural Affairs Department.
Photo credit: Larry Lytle

susan dailey

THE POWER OF UNITY
In collaboration with Mario Echevarria. A mosaic project conceived to help unite and give pride to a neighborhood with a violent past. Community members helped with the visual imagery, posed for figures, assisted with construction, and added their handprints to the back of the mural.
Ceramic mosaic tile, concrete
7' x 15' x 12" (2 m x 5 m x 30 cm)
Photo credit: Amy Boudreau, Western Sky Photography

THE POWER OF UNITY (DETAIL)

susan dailey

TRIBUTE TO THE PIEROTTI CLOWNS
Located in the historic district of Los Alamos, New Mexico, this project was created in honor of a five-man softball team. The team dressed up as clowns and played for 25 years, raising hundreds of thousands of dollars for charity and bringing laughter wherever they went.
Handmade glazed tiles, commercially made mosaic tiles, concrete, stucco base
7' x 22' x 24" (2 m x 7 m x 61 cm)

TRIBUTE TO THE PIEROTTI CLOWNS (DETAIL)

public spaces : learning

linda beaumont

▸ **CIELITO' LINDA**
The Kiosko of San Lucas School, Mexico
Designed and built in collaboration with Steve
Badanes and students from the University of
Washington Architecture School
Mexican tiles, mirror, found objects
15' x 22' x 10' (5 x 7 x 3 m)
Photo credit: Steve Badanes

▾ **CIELITO' LINDA**
Photo credit: Steve Badanes

ericka clark shaw

▴ **THE NATURE AND SEASONS TABLE**
Mill Valley Middle School, California
Working with art students, tables were created to
provide competitive game playing during recess
and after school that did not involve violence. The
students chose the themes and created games for
one to four players.
Handmade ceramic tiles, bas-relief images, mosaic
on concrete
36" (91 cm) diameter

ellen blakeley

▾ MATH MURAL
The Harvey Milk Civil Rights Academy,
San Francisco, California
Students supplied math drawings and problems, which
were incorporated into the larger geometric design.
Tempered glass, plate glass, mixed-media collage,
grout
6' x 12' (2 x 4 m)
Photo credit: Joni West

⩔ MATH MURAL (DETAIL)
Photo credit: Joni West

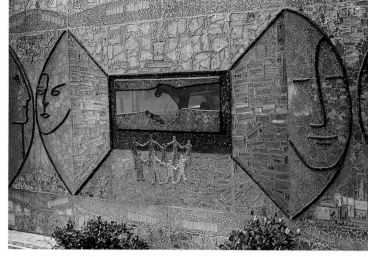

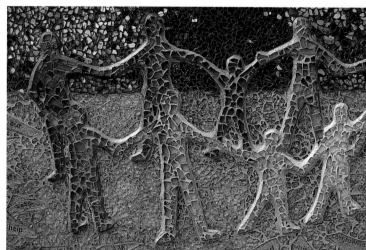

ellen blakeley

⩘ CIVIL RIGHTS—HUMAN RIGHTS MURAL
The Harvey Milk Civil Rights Academy,
San Francisco, California
This final mural was begun shortly before
September 11, 2001, and the project became
a reflection of that tragic day.
Tempered glass, plate glass, mixed-media
collage, grout
6' x 12' (2 x 4 m)
Photo credit: Joni West

▴ CIVIL RIGHTS—HUMAN RIGHTS MURAL
(DETAIL)
Photo credit: Joni West

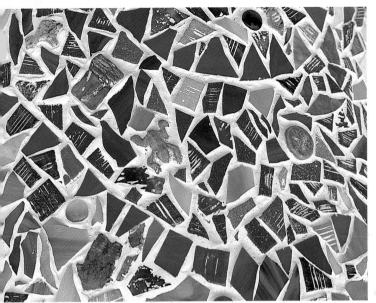

mark soppeland

▲ THE GUARDIAN OF KNOWLEDGE (DETAIL)

▶ THE GUARDIAN OF KNOWLEDGE
Nordia Hills Library, Northfield, Ohio
10,000 pieces of glass with 900 handmade
ceramic animal tiles set in epoxy on a fiberglass
surface over a laminated exterior plywood core
9' 3" (2.7 m)

nina solomon

▶ SPANISH PERIOD MURAL (DETAIL)
Solomon worked as lead artist, with Stacy Stickler
and Alex Camacho, graduate students in landscape
architecture at the University of Arizona.
Photo credit: Dan Solomon

▼ SPANISH PERIOD MURAL
Tucson Museum of Art Education Building and
Courtyard, Tucson, Arizona
Working with the seniors at the Howenstein Magnet
Service Learning High School in Tucson, Arizona,
the Education Building courtyard was renovated,
including four mosaic murals depicting the history
of Tucson.
Handmade stoneware tiles, cement board
34" x 130" x ½" (86 x 330 x 1 cm)
Photo credit: Dan Solomon

donna webb and
joseph blue sky

▲ STAIRWAY TO THE ARTS (DETAIL)
Photo credit: Thomas Webb

◄ STAIRWAY TO THE ARTS
Vern Riffe Center for the Arts, Shawnee State
University, Portsmouth, Ohio
Inspired by a 1849 meteor shower, the mosaic at
the entrance to the school of art reflects the meteors
falling into the local river. Seven golden meteors
were created, causing the patterns of floor ripples.
Ash benches by Thomas Webb are tiled to look
like the riverbank.
Stoneware, ash wood
18' x 18' x 4' (5.5 x 5.5 x 1.2 m)
Photo credit: Thomas Webb

▼ THE FOUNTAIN
Commissioned by the sisters of Theta Phi Alpha, this
piece resides in the central rotunda in the student
union at the University of Akron, Ohio. The quotation,
"Nothing great is ever achieved without much
enduring," is from Catherine of Siena, the patron
saint of the sorority. Thomas Webb created the ash
bench for students to rendezvous. Water streams
over the tiles into an elliptical basin.
8,000 handmade porcelain tiles, ash wood, granite,
stainless steel
8' x 24' x 5' (2.4 x 7.2 x 1.5 m)
Photo credit: Jody Hawk

◄ THE FOUNTAIN (DETAIL)
Photo credit: Jody Hawk

gary monaco

▸ PRAIRIE (DETAIL)

▾ COLORADO
Created for the Southglenn Public Library
A reflection on the beauty of the state of Colorado,
the mural is an enticement for young children to
enjoy their section of the library.
Tile, stained glass.
8' x 16' x 29" (2.4 m x 4.8 m x 74 cm)
Photo credit: Charlie Roy

⯮ COLORADO (DETAIL)
Photo credit: Charlie Roy

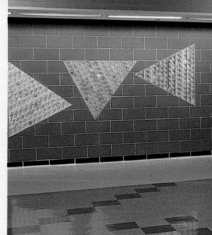

susan tunick

‹ **FOR ALL: THREE TIMES THREE**
Firefighter Christopher A. Santora School, Jackson Heights, Queens, New York
The school is an early learning center designed exclusively for kindergartners, first- and second-graders. For the school's cafeteria, nine large shapes were used to incorporate easily identifiable visual symbols—circles, hexagons, and triangles. The triangles use an ancient wave motif with inserts of fish, shells, and other sea creatures. The circles contained lines form the A.A. Milne poem, "Now We Are Six," and the hexagons focused on objects found in nature—beehives and honeycombs.
Commercial tile from the United Kingdom, the United States, and Germany; antique tile strips; handmade ceramic mosaics
50' (15.2 m)
Photo credit: Peter Mauss/ESTO

▲ **FOR ALL: THREE TIMES THREE (DETAIL)**
Photo credit: Peter Mauss/ESTO

‹ **FOR ALL: THREE TIMES THREE (DETAIL)**
Photo credit: Peter Mauss/ESTO

▼ **FOR ALL: THREE TIMES THREE (DETAIL)**
Photo credit: Peter Mauss/ESTO

david leonard

HACIENDA MOSAICO
Puerto Vallarta, Mexico

▸ **CENA CON PABLO,
POOLSIDE DINING TABLE**
Mexican tiles with utensils
29" x 60" diameter (74 x 152 cm)
Photo credit: Rosa Chavez

▴ **CENA CON PABLO (DETAIL)**

◂ **STUDY IN COLOR (DETAIL)**
Dining table commissioned by Mr. and Mrs.
Earl Lestz
Mexican tiles, copper base
29" x 48" x 48" (74 x 122 x 122 cm)
Photo credit: Rosa Chavez

david leonard

HACIENDA MOSAICO
Puerto Vallarta, Mexico

◄ HERE'S LOOKIN' AT YOU:
DRESSING MIRROR
Mexican tile, glass beads, ceramic face mask, glass objects, wooden gold lamé shoe forms
76" x 34" (193 x 86 cm)
Photo credit: Rosa Chavez

⤢ HERE'S LOOKIN' AT YOU:
DRESSING MIRROR (DETAIL)
Photo credit: Rosa Chavez

▲ GARDEN WALL WITH A FOUNTAIN
Mexican tiles, dichroic glass, beach glass
9' x 20' (2.7 x 6 m)
Photo credit: Rosa Chavez

◄ GARDEN WALL WITH A FOUNTAIN (DETAIL)
Photo credit: Rosa Chavez

josie martin

THE GIANTS HOUSE—LINTON
Akaroa, Christchurch, New Zealand

▼ EMILE, DANCING WITH HER TUTU SKIRT
AS A TABLE
Tiles, broken china shards, concrete sculptural forms
Construction assistant: Jonathan Hall
Photo credit: Jonathan Hall

▼ FLIGHTS OF FANCY: SEATS IN THE GARDEN
Tiles, broken china shards, concrete sculptural forms
Construction assistant: Jonathan Hall
Photo credit: Jonathan Hall

josie martin

THE GIANTS HOUSE—LINTON
Akaroa, Christchurch, New Zealand

▲ BLUEBELLA IN GARDEN
Tiles, broken china shards, concrete sculptural form
Construction assistant: Jonathan Hall
Photo credit: Jonathan Hall

▲ PLACE DES AMIS
Tiles, broken china shards, concrete sculptural forms
16½' x 29' 7" (5 x 9 m)
Construction assistant: Jonathan Hall
Photo credit: Jonathan Hall

josie martin

THE GIANTS HOUSE—LINTON
Akaroa, Christchurch, New Zealand

◂ MOSAIC WALKWAY IN THE GARDEN
Tiles, broken china shards
Construction assistant: Jonathan Hall
Photo credit: Jonathan Hall

▾ THE NOSEY PARKERS LOOKING OVER
PLACE DES AMIS
Tiles, broken china shards, concrete sculptural forms
Construction assistant: Jonathan Hall
Photo credit: Jonathan Hall

josie martin

THE GIANTS HOUSE—LINTON
Akaroa, Christchurch, New Zealand

◂◂ ROSA WITH FANTAIL
Tiles, broken china shards, concrete sculptural forms
Construction assistant: Jonathan Hall
Photo credit: Jonathan Hall

◂ RUBY DELICIOUS AND JIMMY BY THE POND
Tiles, broken china shards, concrete sculptural forms
Construction assistant: Jonathan Hall
Photo credit: Jonathan Hall

sylvia seret

INN OF THE FIVE GRACES
Santa Fe, New Mexico

▸ **SUITE 19: BATHTUB AND SINK AREA**
Broken pottery from Puebla, Mexico, and Jaipur,
India; blue and white talavera field tile; broken
Turkish vases
6' x 7' (1.8 x 2.1 m)
Photo credit: Don Marr

▾ **SUITE 19: BATHTUB AND SINK AREA
(DETAIL)**
Photo credit: Don Marr

sylvia seret

INN OF THE FIVE GRACES
Santa Fe, New Mexico

◂ **SUITE 20: BATH (DETAIL)**
Photo credit: Don Marr

▴ **SUITE 20: WETBAR**
Talavera tile, broken pottery, Fiestaware plates
and cup handles
4½" x 5' (1.4 x 1.5 m)
Photo credit: Simon Mehalek

sylvia seret

INN OF THE FIVE GRACES
Santa Fe, New Mexico

▸ SUITE 22: BATH (DETAIL)

⯆ SUITE 22: WINDOW (DETAIL)

▾ SUITE 22: SINK (DETAIL)

sylvia seret

INN OF THE FIVE GRACES
Santa Fe, New Mexico

▴ SUITE 21: KASHMIR BATH (DETAIL)
Talavera field tile, broken Jaipur checkerboard vase
collection, turquoise pottery, clear glass chips, gold
mosaic chips
Photo credit: Don Marr

directory of artists

LYNN ADAMO
117

Our House Tile Design
942 NE Third Avenue
Hillsboro, OR 97124
United States
Phone: 503.640.0660
lynn@ourhousedesign.com
www.ourhousedesign.com

AHMED AGRAMA
95

Horseshoe Canyon Ceramics
2458 Horseshoe Canyon Road
Los Angeles, CA 90046
United States
Phone: 323.848.9710
aagrama@harmonygold.com

AKOMENA
121

Akomena Spazio Mosaico
Via Ponte della Vecchia 27
San Zaccaria
48020, Ravenna
Italy
Phone: 011.39.0544.554700
akomena@akomena.com
www.akomena.com

KAREN AMI
107

Mudhouse Studio
3841 North Ashland Avenue
Chicago, IL 60613
United States
Phone: 773.975.7522
mudhousestudio@aol.com
www.mudhousestudio.com

TINA AMIDON
115

Mixed Media Home & Garden
438 35 Street
Richmond, CA 94805
United States
Phone: 510.237.6986
tinaamidon@earthlink.net

TWYLA ARTHUR
96

2007 West Summit Avenue
San Antonio, TX 78201
United States
Phone: 210.735.3450
twylaa@earthlink.net

CANDACE BAHOUTH
104

The Dell
Weir Lane-Pilton
Somerset BA4 4BS
United Kingdom
Phone: 44.01749.890.433

**SOLOMON BASSOFF
DOMENICA MOTTARELA**
12–15

Faducci
P.O. Box 923
North San Juan, CA 95960
United States
Phone: 530.292.3857
info@faducci.com
www.faducci.com

EDWIN STUART BAXTER
16–19

Dhangin Taman
Tirtagangga, Karangasem
Bali 80852
Indonesia
Phone: 62.363.22521
esbaxter@indo.net.id
www.baxtermosaicart.com

LINDA BEAUMONT
111, 128

Truefaux
5294 Lola Lane
Langley, WA 98260
United States
Phone: 360.321.5731
beaululu@earthlink.net

**TRACY GRAVIER BELL AND
ROBIN OLDHAM FRANKLIN**
113

Smashing Times®
308 Preston Royal Shopping
Center
Dallas, TX 75230
United States
Phone: 214.363.2088
info@smashingtimes.com
www.smashingtimes.com

JOANNE BERKE
105

2548 Fickle Hill Road
Arcata, CA 95521
United States
Phone: 707.822.8760
jbb1@humboldt.edu

CAROL BEVILACQUA
108, 115

Duro-Design
1937 Cedar Street
Berkeley, CA 94710
United States
Phone: 510.204.9665
carol.bev@sbcglobal.net

ELLEN BLAKELEY
129

Ellen Blakeley Studio
874 Pauline Court
Santa Rosa, CA 95401
United States
Phone: 707.573.1709
bhotsand@aol.com
www.ellenblakeley.com

JUDI BRENNAN
20–25

Clay Art Studios
Gallery & Mosaics
255 Mapara Road
Acacia Bay
Taupo, New Zealand
Phone: 64.07.378.2962
mosaics@clayartstudio.co.nz
www.clayartstudio.co.nz

DANIELA CARAVITA
118, 122-123

Via Reale, 308
Mezzano
48010, Ravenna
Italy
Phone: 39.0544.523293
mosart@mosart.it
www.mosart.it

JULIE CHARLES
112

Crackpot Mosaics
18 Florentina Street
Seattle, WA 98109
United States
Phone: 206.691.3000
juliecharles@yahoo.com
www.crackpotmosaics.com

IRINA CHARNY
98, 100

IC Mosaics
19502 Sierra Santo Road
Irvine, CA 92612
United States
Phone: 949.823.9219
irina@icmosaics.com
www.icmosaics.com

SUSAN DAILEY
127

South Hollywood Studios
P.O. Box 1166
Laporte, CO 80535
United States
Skdailey@juno.com
www.artscomm.org/skdailey

MARCELO DE MELO
26–31

Edinburgh Sculpture Workshop
25 Hawthornvale
Edinburgh, Scotland EH6 4JT
marcmcmelo@yahoo.co.uk
www.mosaicable.co.uk

JULIA DI BIASI
99

mezza matta
San Francisco, CA
United States
Phone: 415.699.3846
julia@mezzamatta.com
www.mezzamatta.com

GINA DOMINGUEZ
116

Snapshot Mosaics
1532 Excelsior Avenue
Oakland, CA 94602
United States
Phone: 510.531.9755
gina@snapshotmosaics.com
www.snapshotmosaics.com

LINDA EDEIKEN
32–37

Mad Platter Beaded Mosaics
United States
Phone: 858.459.8611
mosaics@san.rr.com
www.madplattermosaics.com

MICHELLE ENUS
38–41

Creative Mosaix
6915 Camrose Drive
Los Angeles, CA 90068
United States
Phone: 310.963.9898
creativemosaix@earthlink.net
www.creativemosaix.com

CHERYL EVANS
101

Mosaic Court Designs
859 Mosaic Court
Gahanna, OH 43230
United States
Phone: 614.855.1859
revans5@columbus.rr.com

GEORGE FISHMAN
106

103 NE 99 Street
Miami Shores, FL 33138
United States
Phone: 305.758.1141
gfmosaics@bellsouth.net

ROSÂNGELA K. GASPARIN
117

AMPAP
Rua Costa Rica, 770 ap 302-
Bacacheri
Curitiba Paraná CEP 82510-180
Brazil
Phone: 55.41.257.3237
plinioerosangela@uol.com.br

**ALLISON GOLDENSTEIN
AND LESLEY PROVENZANO**
120

Mixed Up Mosaics
29 West 17th Street, 2nd Floor
New York, NY 10011
United States
Phone: 212.243.9944
mosaicdesigner@aol.com
www.mixed-upmosaics.com

SARIT PILZ GRANIT
95

#1 Neve Reim St.
Ramit Hasharon 47265
Israel
Phone: 972.3.5408399
agranit@bezeqint.net

PATTIE GREY
111

338 Butterfield Road
San Anselmo, CA 94960
United States
Phone: 415.459.4721
epgrey@aol.com
www.pattigrey.com

DIDIER GUEDJ
42–47

Mosaics All the Way
815 ½ Solono Avenue
Los Angeles, CA 90012
United States
Phone: 323.221.9104
mosaicsatw@earthlink.net
www.mosaicsalltheway.com/

DEBBY HAGAR
126

Debby Hagar Art Tiles
1621 Buckeye Road
Knoxville, TN 37919
United States
Phone: 865.690.6888
ArtTile@mindspring.com
www.debbyhagar.com

XUAN MY HO
110

Swan Mosaic
139 Forest View Road
Woodside, CA 94062-4514
United States
Phone: 650.529.1378
myxuanho@hotmail.com
www.swanmosaic.com

GINA HUBLER
102

Design Impact
P.O. Box 490176
Key Biscayne, FL 33149
United States
Phone: 800.557.3444
gina@designimp.com
www.designimp.com

LUCINDA JOHNSON
48–51

Anima Ceramic Design
220 N. Zapata Highway, Room 11
Laredo, TX 78043-4427
United States
Phone: 415.155.8002
anima@mcn.org
www.animatile.com

NATSU KAJI
103

Tile Shop Gaudi
Gosyogaoka, 3-10-3
Moriya shi Ibaraki
Japan
Phone: 81.0297.71.6888
na-tsu-ko@japan.email.ne.jp

SONIA KING
108, 118, 124

Sonia King Mosaics
1023 Sarasota Circle
Dallas, TX 75223
United States
Phone: 214.824.5854
sonia@mosaicworks.com
www.mosaicworks.com

DAVID LEONARD
134–135

graceleonard@yahoo.com
vallarta-mosaicart.com

GORDAN MANDICH
113

10/261 Heidelberg Road
Northcote
3070 Melbourne, Victoria
Australia
Phone: 61.03.9486.7168
mandich@iprimus.com.au
www.mandichmosaics.com

JOSIE MARTIN
136–137

The Giants House–Linton
68 Rue Balguerie
Akaroa
Christchurch, New Zealand
Phone: 64.03.304.7501
josiemartin@paradise.net.nz
www.linton.co.nz

SHERRY McCALL
95

McCall's Stonemosaic, Inc.
1185 Chat Holley Road
Santa Rosa Beach, FL 32459
United States
Phone: 850.267.2790
smccall@stonemosaic.com
www.stonemosaic.com

LAURIE MIKA
107

Mika Arts
1540 Tzena Way
Encinitas, CA 92024
United States
Phone: 760.436.3855
laurie@mikaarts.com
www.mikaarts.com

GARY MONACO
132

4623 South Robb Street
Littleton, CO 80127
United States
Phone: 303.979.3848
monacogh@aol.com

MARY ANN MOORE
118

7777 South May Avenue
Oklahoma City, Oklahoma
73159
United States
Phone: 405.682.7558

RICHARD MOSS
52-57

Equipment of Culture
95 Saint James Avenue
Holyoke, MA 01040-2322
United States
Phone: 413.534.3555
rm@eofc.com
www.eofc.com

CLAUDIA NAGY
106

Nagy-Arts
United States
Phone: 212.941.7535
mosaic@nagy-arts.com
www.nagy-arts.com

HARUO NAKABAYASHI
96, 110

Mosaic Atelier Naka
468-22 Kizawa
Oyama-shi, Tochigi-Ken
Japan
Phone: 011.81.0285.24.0119
atelienaka@msn.com

LUCIANA NOTTURNI
109

Officina del Mosaico
via Arno, 13
48100, Ravenna
Italy
Phone: 39.0544.36192
mosaic@sira.it
www.mosaicschool.com

LUCIO ORSONI
58–61

Domus Orsoni
Cannaregio 1045
30121 Venezia
Italy
Phone: 011.39.041.2759538
info@domusorsoni
www.domusorsoni.it

BEA PEREIRA
116

AMPAP
Rue Epitácio Pessoa, 103
Curitiba, Paraná CEP 82530-270
Brazil
Phone: 55.41.262.1602
deposito@depositodaordem.
com.br

LINDA PRINCE
113

Partake
P.O. Box 11
Banksia
Sydney NSW 2216
Australia
Phone: 61.02.9567.3917
linda@partake.com.au
www.partake.com.au

SANTIAGO RODRIGUEZ
119

Emblemata Mosaics
2407 Harrison Street, #3
San Francisco, CA 94110
United States
Phone: 415.206.1388
santiago@frjtzfries.com

SYLVIA SERET
118, 138–139

Seret & Sons Rugs & Furnishings
224 Galisteo Street
Santa Fe, NM 87501
United States
Phone: 505.988.9151
helix@cybermesa.com
www.fivegraces.com

ILANA SHAFIR
112

Kapstadt Street 2
Ashkelon 78406
Israel
Phone: 972.8.6732879
artilana@012.net.il
www.shafirart.com

ERICKA CLARK SHAW
128

E. Clark Ceramics
53 Laurel Grove Avenue
Kentfield, CA 94904
United States
Phone: 415.460.1645
eclarkceramics@hotmail.com

MINDY SIMBRAT
104

Murphy, NC 28906
United States
ks32250@aol.com

LILLIAN SIZEMORE
97

Lillian Sizemore Design
P.O. Box 31899
San Francisco, CA 94131-0899
United States
lillian@sfmosaic.com
www.sfmosaic.com

LAUREL SKYE
62–67

Laurel Skye Designs
948 11th Street
Arcata, CA 95521
United States
Phone: 707.822.6677
laurelskye@sbcglobal.net
http://homepage.mac.com/
laurelskye/

NINA SOLOMON
130

Ilitzky Solomon Studios, LLC
1817 West Northview Avenue
Phoenix, AZ 85021
United States
Phone: 602.995.0804
ninasolomon@yahoo.com
www.ninasolomon.com

MARK SOPPELAND
130

The Odd Museum
576 Fairhill Drive
Akron, OH 44313-5406
United States
Phone: 330.873.9555
msoppeland@uakron.edu

ROBYN SPENCER-CROMPTON
68–71

Spencer Crompton Studio &
Gardens
4367 Raymonde Way
Santa Rosa, CA 95404
United States
Phone: 707.542.6601
RobynSpenc@aol.com

JUDY STONE
72–77

Mosaic Art & Design
6112 44th Place
Riverdale Park, MD 20737
United States
Phone: 301.537.9115
judystone@mosaic.net
www.mosaic.net

**ROBERT STOUT AND
STEPHANIE JURS**
96, 125

Twin Dolphin Mosaics
Via Bartolini, 8
48100 Ravenna
Italy
Phone: 39.0544.456.345
contact@twindolphinmosaics.com
www.twindolphinmosaics.com

CRAIGIE S. SUCCOP
78–81

Turtle Cove Mosaics
Turtle Cove
23944 Porters Creek Lane
Saint Michaels, MD 21663
United States
Phone: 410.745.2879
craigie@intercom.net

FILIPPO TAZZARI
97

Opus snc
Via Oxilia 9
20127 Milano
Italy
Phone: 39.02.28510282
filippo@infoopus.com
www.infoopus.com

KAREN THOMPSON
82–87

Archetile
694 Tennessee Street
San Francisco, CA 94107
United States
Phone: 415.647.1594
archetile@comcast.net

ENZO TINARELLI
105

Via Farini 16
54031 Carrara (MS)
Italy
Phone: 39.0585.55560
enzo.tinarelli@virgilio.it

KII TOYOHARU
119

2771-3 Sakahama, Inagi-shi
Tokyo
Japan
Phone: 81.042.331.5719
kii@ttv.ne.jp

LAUREL TRUE
88–93

True Mosaics
2142 8th Avenue
Oakland, CA 94606
United States
Phone: 510.437.9899
laurel@truemosaics.com
www.truemosaics.com

SUSAN TUNICK
133

771 West End Avenue, 10E
New York, NY 10025
United States

JOHN T. UNGER
117

John T. Unger Studio
3014 South M-66 Highway
Mancelona, MI 49659
United States
Phone: 231.584.2710
john@johntunger.com
www.johntunger.com

STEVEN VELLA
114

P.O. Box 734
Darlinghurst, Sydney
N.S.W. 1300
Australia
Phone: 011.61.2.9557.9307
stevenvella@optusnet.com.au

**DONNA WEBB AND
JOSEPH BLUE SKY**
131

69 Edgerton Road
Akron, OH 44303
United States
Phone: 330.869.8644
dwebb@uakron.edu

**LOUIS G. WEINER AND
CINDY D. JONES**
95, 114

Jacob Jones Mosaics
P.O. Box 6826
Big Bear Lake, CA 92315
United States
Phone: 909.866.5409
info@jacobjones.com
www.jacobjones.com

DEB CARLSON WIGHT
99, 103

320 Fuller Drive
Bergheim, TX 78004
United States
Phone: 210.508.6750
mozaicdesigns@yahoo.com

SUSAN WINK
125

309 North Missouri Avenue
Roswell, NM 88201
United States
Phone: 505.627.7206
winksusan@hotmail.com

NANCY WITTELS
111

Rolling Fog Design
P.O. Box 700512
San Jose, CA 95170
United States
Phone: 408.253.3900
nancy@rollingfog.com
www.rollingfog.com

BETTY ROSEN ZIFF
126

P.O. Box 452873
Los Angeles, CA 90045
United States
Phone: 310.338.1555
brosenziff@comcast.net
www.bettyrosenziff.com

about the author

JoAnn Locktov is a development and marketing consultant in the visual and performing arts. She is a former advisory board member of the Society of American Mosaic Artists. In 2004, she chaired the 3rd annual SAMA Conference, which took place in San Francisco, California. She is the coauthor of *The Art of Mosaic Design* (Rockport, 1998).

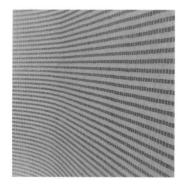

acknowledgments

I wish to thank all of the mosaic artists who submitted their wonderful work for this book, allowing their art to be open to inspection. I value my mosaic artist friends, Stephanie Jurs and Robert Stout, who never cease to amaze me with their artistry, knowledge, and willingness to help; Robin Brett who is always so gracious and full of information; and Sonia King for being the inimitable Sonia King.

Joe Taylor and Sheila Menzies, the founders of the Tile Heritage Foundation, buoy me with their infectious joy and support of mosaic art. A very belated thank you to Susan McDowell for encouraging a seed to grow, which is now this book you hold in your hands. My deepest appreciation to Mark Farrell, who supplied the comedic relief that every author should be so lucky to have.

Mary Ann Hall and Betsy Gammons, my editors at Rockport, have been inspiring sources of wisdom and patience during the entire process of creating this book. My agent, Linda Allen, has become my mentor in life and a friend I cherish. Finally, my family—always in my heart—as they continue to allow me to indulge in my passion for mosaics.